Iain Sinclair is a writer and filmmaker based in East London. His books include the novels *Downriver* (1991) and *Radon Daughters* (1994), and the speculative documentaries, *Lights Out for the Territory* (1997), *London Orbital* (2002) and *Hackney, That Rose-Red Empire* (2009). His most recent book, *Black Apples of Gower*, was an unexpected return to the country of his birth, Wales. He is working on the endgame of a long sequence, *The Last London*.

Fenced Horizons, 2005, oil on canvas, by Partou Zia

ALCHEMY

–

Joanna Kavenna, Gabriel Josipovici,
Benjamin Markovits, Partou Zia,
Anakana Schofield

–

with an introduction by
Iain Sinclair

Notting Hill Editions

Published in 2016
by Notting Hill Editions Ltd
Widworthy Barton Honiton Devon EX14 9JS

Designed by FLOK Design, Berlin, Germany
Typeset by CB editions, London

Printed and bound
by Memminger MedienCentrum, Memmingen, Germany

A CIP record for this book
is available from the British Library

ISBN 978-1-910749-16-6

www.nottinghilleditions.com

Contents

Iain Sinclair

– Introduction: The Great Work –

> The alchemical operation consisted essentially in
> separating the prima materia, the so-called chaos, into
> the active principle, the soul, and the passive principle,
> the body, which were then reunited in personified form
> in the coniunnctio or 'chemical wedding'.
> – C. G. Jung, *Alchemical Studies*

T he risk in exposing our sources of inspiration,
where the primal spark comes from and how it
is transmuted, is of tearing the wings from a butterfly
to explain flight. The impulse to write, to put a shape
on chaos, is the neurosis that defines us, that allows us
to find credit in failure: poetry as a sickness vocation.
But then, as the various contributors to the collection
published as *Alchemy* discover, there is relief in that
provocative metaphor. Alchemy, existing on the hinge
of the medieval and pre-modern worlds, offers a certain
dignity of process to initiates of language; the branded
ones who are prepared to work and rework, in darkness, by instinct, to achieve the faintest sliver of golden
light. It slips through their fingers like a mercury spill.
The story. The innocent confession. The lie that persuades. The comforting illusion of achievement in the
accidental arrangement of words on a page.

The *Alchemy* writers identify with an intensely local force field known as the Self, while appreciating that its borders, through homeopathic doses of loss or hurt or love, can burst; so that, in the instant of composition, there is no division between individual consciousness and the world at large. Vision is the name we give to that absolute. The thing that can't be forced, prostituted or sold short. And herein lies the paradox and the challenge for the five chosen witnesses, who are privileged to write themselves out of the trap, the Faustian contract, by way of personal anecdote, strategic revelation or hopeful punt in the dark. The belief is declared several times in these essays that the natural world has its established mechanisms, suns will rise and rise again. We labour in that expectation, blackest night before dawn. Disillusion, anomie, betrayal are accepted as necessary tolls for access to the Great Work.

Gabriel Josipovici quotes Beckett, somebody had to: '*Bon qu'a ça.*' The condemned author – condemned to live – puts words on paper because it is all that he or she can do. Foolish to comment any further. But now comment is required. Comment has been solicited. 'The writing is painfully aware,' Josipovici says, 'of the fact that the rhetoric both reinforces and undermines the anguish.'

In playing the game, feinting at a posthumous explanation for what is, in effect, an electrochemical seizure, a sudden thickening of the tongue, a suspension of conditioned reflexes, the essayist finds relief in identification with terrain, some elective topography capable of bearing the weight of the metaphor that must be imposed upon it. Vision is out there and we will walk, hobble, swim or crawl, to find it. The special place might, for Partou Zia, be a flint field at the end of the land. A soft-focus garden running down to the Thames for Joanna Kavenna. A busy urban road for Gabriel Josipovici. An aircraft coming down on a motorway embankment for Anakana Schofield. Geography is destiny, but 'reality' is a tight bone cage: the cell of the skull from which consoling sets are conjured. The writer's task is to recognise the place that is writing you; triggering the voices, giving you permission to continue.

I began my own long and frustrating engagement with London by quoting from *A Vision* by W. B. Yeats. And I've never, in more than forty years, found good reason to go beyond that. 'The living can assist the imagination of the dead.' We are ventriloquised, confirmed in our fantasies. This is what we must do and we are doing it. 'To drift into the poetic is in itself work,' Zia says. Kavenna shares my belief that writing is rewriting. We receive and record the stories that press in upon us, across the boundaries of sleep and mortality. 'I was troubled by bad dreams and these had an intensely tactile and auditory quality, and often seeped into the ensuing day, like a miasma. In my dreams the dead were alive.' It is not Kavenna talking to us, it is her character, her creature, Anthony Yorke, who is one thing here and another in a different text. He is a blocked writer, a teacher – and an actor. He luxuriates in taxonomies of failure. He resents his role in this slippery production. 'This is nothing and everything, all at once.'

With intimations of a double displacement, separation from homeland and from physical well-being, Zia recognises her exile as a highway. 'Barren country roads crowned by a ribbon of mathematically-arranged wires that stitch earth-horizons with the wide sky. Hours spent in bed reading, my only solace. Outside is alien, and I am too vulnerable to venture forth.' The cold English sea is a cinema of memory in which the memories are not her own. The road is a prediction, running from past to future. 'There are those who will scowl at the pavement as they tread their isolated path, determined to keep their starved souls in the deprived element of spiritual poverty.' Along the stripped spine of a moorland track, the unresting dead are the only pilgrims.

What excites me, as a reader of the five texts, is how molecular reactions fizz between them to stitch a single hydra-headed, argumentative entity. It really does feel that none of these pieces could have been written in the form they have settled on without the existence of the others. Sometimes the forward momentum of the narrative is grudging, sometimes it flows with the reckless inevitability of a river in spate.

Zia's road of exile, out there in the far west, tapping sources common to earlier migrants, such as W. S. Graham, D. H. Lawrence, Mary Butts, dissolves into Josipovici's tramp from Brixton to New Cross: 'so endless, so rundown and desperate that it becomes purgatorial.' Moral exhaustion opens a grunge portal on the horrors of Francis Bacon's painting of a vomiting man in a sealed room. The description brought me back to my first experience of London in 1962, when I made a number of hikes from Electric Avenue, Brixton, to the great Bacon retrospective at the old Tate Gallery on Millbank. Prominence in the show was given to Bacon's reworking of Van Gogh's *Painter on the Road to Tarascon*; a molten rendering that became the marker for a lifetime of burdened trudging, of too many days walking out to write.

The condition of exile or tolerated otherness, defined by two of the *Alchemy* authors as a road, becomes an apprenticeship in migration for Benjamin Markovits. He leaves the USA for a season, trying out as a basketball player in Germany. Reading his finessed report, with its deceptively conversational style, we soon understand that the real apprenticeship, the bullet that can't be dodged, is to become a professional writer.

All the presentations have as their most immediate and defining quality the acceptance, reluctant or otherwise, of confrontation with the challenge of the commission: 'writing about the mysterious process of transmuting experience into art, using a life-changing event to trigger the creative process.' In every case, we register the writer at the desk, gazing out of a window, moving around the house, firing up a start, then pausing to question the process; wriggling against the necessity of labouring to a pre-ordained conclusion, labouring for money. An imaginative flourish will stall into reverie, into reaching for a supporting quote from some respected predecessor in the game: Virginia Woolf, Kafka, Herman Melville, Borges, Wittgenstein. Otherwise, writers must become teachers. Kavenna: 'Yes, Anthony was also a tutor.' Josipovici: 'My frustration went on through my two years of graduate work and my first two years as an Assistant Lecturer in the newly formed University of Sussex.' Markovits: 'I've been teaching now for about ten years and there's a line I use on students to describe what seems to me difficult about writing . . . But novels are about things happening, and so when we start writing fiction there's this gap we have to bridge between the uneventfulness of our experience and the drama that we think is supposed to take place on the page.'

Where then is the truth, the true imprint of experience? Where is the author in all this? W. G. Sebald and Roberto Bolaño tease us with apparent versions of themselves in fictions that behave like reportage, or essays as playful as novels. We make those identifications at our peril. '*Real*,' Bolaño wrote, in *A Little Lumpen Novelita*, 'only stands for a different kind of unreality.'

In a book called *Hackney, That Rose-Red Empire*, I used the devices of fiction to test a mythology of place made from hard evidence and the traces of writers who had worked the territory in previous generations. I studded the story, to ghost at a sort of authenticity, with a series of transcribed interviews that I edited into seamless monologues. One of the interviewees, reporting on her past as a weekend ecstasy raver, asked me to disguise her identity. I used her words but tweaked certain details to make the young woman into an architect whose thesis was to keep everything theoretical. 'No structure that can be commissioned, she asserted, was worth making. The aim of human existence was to do absolutely nothing, gracefully. Any intervention was doomed to make things worse.'

Soon after the book was published, I was approached by an architecture magazine asking for contact details, so that they could compose a feature about this exciting newcomer. I had to confess that I'd made her up. 'Impossible,' said the man on the end of the phone. 'I met her at a party in Shoreditch last Wednesday.'

The only fiction, as the *Alchemy* collective reveals, is that they are writing fiction. The element of self-interrogation is more fabulous than the more apparently contrived episodes. I believe in Joanna Kavenna's troubled author with the halting visions that he is trying to extract from his projection of a phantom female on the lawn. The absurdity carries absolute conviction.

I wonder about the downbeat adventures of Benjamin Markovits in Germany, even though they could come straight from a recovered letter home. I believe the elegantly measured opening of 'The Difficult Question' by Anakana Schofield: the rain, the red Clarks sandals, the dead father who refuses to save himself in the crashed plane. The authorial voice has the confidence of Bolaño or Sebald – which is to say that we invest our trust in the skill of the storyteller. And we grow uneasy when the magician tries to explain the trick.

So here is a true story. My wife told it to me on her return from a day's outing to Oxford. Why was she there? I was at home in Hackney, sitting at the desk where I am sitting now, niggling at another commission, another rapidly approaching deadline. There was no time to look out of the window, but I could hear pigeons massing on the tiles. Squirrels headbutting speckled glass. Recently arrived parakeets screeching from tree to tree.

Anna goes, early, into the hotel where she has her meeting, wondering if there is time for coffee or a drink. Someone she recognises is established at a table with her laptop. *Is it?* The woman with the busy screen, fingers flying across the keyboard, is a writer. She comes here to this commercial space, not to a library or a coffee shop, because the atmosphere feels right, it's not oppressive. Most of the passerines are tourists or business folk.

I am interrupted at my desk, to hear the stop-start, digressive movements of the episode. As it is recounted. As it is remade into a serviceable anecdote. The other writer in the Oxford hotel is also stalled, but she says that she's happy to join Anna for a drink. Two commissions are put on hold. *Can I guess who the woman was?* I don't have to try, Anna tells me: Joanna Kavenna. I wonder, now, if Kavenna was working on 'Realia', her piece for this book? Does Anna's intervention cast even the palest shadow on Kavenna's text? 'For some reason Anthony had put his invented woman in an invented house by his invented version of the Thames – and this was why he was in Oxford.'

Kavenna writes about Virginia Woolf 'refusing the "reality" of others'. A place, a set, let us propose the lobby or the bar of a hotel in Oxford, a former bank. There is a theme, in the stories written by women, about bereavement. The drama begins after their fathers die: as fiction, as fiction derived from an actual trauma. Dark forebodings, paradoxically, bring a sharper light to the landscape. To the road of exile, the airport runway, the dead path down which ghosts shuffle. To validate the story, I would have to cook up the tension. Who was my wife meeting? Was the writer composing a blackmail letter to a former tutor? Had she drifted into an episode of *Morse*? Were these modest coincidences a blip in the space-time continuum? Did any of it *really* happen?

Five writers deliver. Five writers invoke other

writers, a communality of purpose. Five writers make concrete the dream of place. Partou Zia begins by quoting Jung. Her essay, taken from a longer work, 'The Notebooks of Eurydice', has an overwhelming sensitivity to sound and smell, to the loss of her country of origin and her integration into the far west of England. Language becomes light. 'It is Light that varies our seeing senses, our emotions . . . TRUST, TRUST, TRUST.' But light is also the authorial voice, when it is detached from the page; it is the necessary element for which five very different writers are in quest. 'We can safely call the light the central mystery of philosophical alchemy,' said Jung.

Joanna Kavenna

– Realia* –

* noun: objects and material from everyday life.
ORIGIN 1950s: from late Latin, neuter plural (used as a
noun) of *realis* 'relating to things' (see *real*)

I

S he was walking back to the house, carrying a letter, her dress swishing on the lawn, the sound of wind in the trees around her. Birds were wheeling in the sky, flying from the eaves of the house . . . and back again . . .

She was walking with the swallows (*more specific*) wheeling in the sky and the sound of the water lapping the banks of the river, old old river, wending its watery way (*redundant*) towards the greasy old city (*old, old too many olds...*)

She was walking . . .
Water shining in the sun
Glinting
(*Glinting? Shining?*)
She was feeling . . .

She was walking with the birds twittering in the trees,

1

nature burgeoning around her, somewhere, elsewhere, and as she walked she wondered –

She thought . . .

She waited patiently for someone to give her something to think or feel –

OH GOD said the novelist, Anthony Yorke.

A fly was buzzing at the window, so Anthony went to open it.

Go away, he said to the fly. *Or I'll kill you.*

The fly went away, out of the window and across the cloud-fractured sky –

Anthony sat down at the desk again, and waited – he observed his character, shimmering within, elsewhere, out there – inside – his computer shimmered, and she was lit in gaudy nothingness –

The woman was waiting – in her swishy dress, letter in her hand, the sun in her eyes – she was stranded on the grass, expectant, unreal, completely unreal, growing more unreal by the moment – fading, fading before his eyes and becoming even translucent – the grass fading too –

Unreality was descending, like flakes of soot, across the garden –

Not this again, said Anthony Yorke.

What was she feeling? How the hell was he meant to know? Perhaps her mind was as blank as the blue sky above her? As blank as the backlit page before him? Perhaps her mind was full of thoughts he could never hope to fathom, she was swishing along thinking in a way he would never understand even if he spent five years trying to imagine it . . . She was rich and swishy and idle, wandering idly through The Past, how was he meant to know what rich-idle-swishy women thought in The Past anyway?

He shook his head. The woman waited in the garden, her swishy (*satin?*) skirt, some skirt that swished, swishing as she walked. The letter in her hand . . .

Should I open the letter? she thought, or didn't think. Didn't think at all?

Surely she's going to open the letter? thought Anthony. Who doesn't open a letter? Some things aren't relative, surely? Surely everyone gets a letter and rips it right open?

Of course, he said to himself, and to the antiseptic room, a room with blank walls, a flat-packed desk and chair, a suitcase, some boxes – as if he was pretending he didn't really live here. And yet, of course, he did. He lived here for reasons that were painful and improbable. (Lost love, his wife hated him. His ex-wife, of course, he had to remember.)

The woman waited. Perhaps she thought he was taking his time.

The woman waited in her sunny garden.

She waited and then like some screen saver, one of those screen savers that freezes and then unfreezes as you contemplate the off-white walls of a rented room, she unfroze again. She went off walking, in the garden. Of the house. The house with a garden that went all the way down to the river. The River Thames. For some reason Anthony had put his invented woman in an invented house by his invented version of the Thames – and this was why he was in Oxford. This was why – he was here, trying to divine the thoughts of an unreal character, and trying to make them sound real, even though they were not real at all. Anyway it is impossible to know the thoughts of others, he knew. He knew that. Of course, he had never literally squatted inside someone's head, listening to their inner thoughts. The whole thing was impossible, and yet he was trying to make it sound realistic. It had to be realistic. He was a realist novelist, after all. He liked the realist novel. He loved realism. He was as devoutly realist as the next man or woman. He wanted to describe, plausibly and convincingly, the life of a woman living in The Past (1892, he had decided, randomly) and – in the present moment (or in the present of his invented reality) – walking in an immaculately researched and convincingly relayed historical garden, walking, and holding a letter, feeling – feeling . . .

Then it started again. This sick sense that he didn't know what she was feeling at all.

So Anthony Yorke went onto the street. To fail outdoors, in the sunshine, is more wholesome than to fail indoors. He hoped that was true. He walked along, passing a lamppost, passing a child bawling at its mother –

He passed metal railings one by one –

He passed Keble College, the Pitt Rivers museum, he stumbled –

A crack in the pavement . . . Better not fall into the crack . . . He passed the crack, tiptoed round the edge –

He passed a weird little glowing green man, suspended aloft, telling him he could walk – he walked –

He passed a few people he didn't know, a few more –

He passed the drifting dust, dust that drifted in the air and drifted into his lungs, he breathed dust –

He passed Trinity College where some student-kids were sprawled on the grass –

Oh gather ye rosebuds, he said under his breath –
Soon you'll be like me, and I'll be – where ?

Another day passed.

The planet wobbled on its axis and some people died and some were born and some nano-particles rearranged themselves, and invisible chemical reactions inside his body allowed Anthony to continue – one more day –

Another day and so Anthony sat back down, at his desk again, the clouds passing the window, time moving on and on, time like an unseen creature sliding towards him, coming to lick him into oblivion – he sat at his desk –

Back, back monster Time –

And he wrote –

She moved through the garden, she moved in her shiny diaphanous bustle dress, she moved her legs and arms, she looked up at the sky and saw the clouds moving and she felt time all around her, moving her along –

In Non-Real Land – she moved along anyway, in The Unreal Created World of Antony Yorke – she moved along –

She pursed her lips into an –

O . . .

Oh

God.

I am not Real, she said.

She stood in the garden, lifted her head to the sky and –

She shouted

But I'm not REAL!

You fool, Yorke . . .

Why did you birth me, and yet I am not real?

Then she put her head in her hands and wept.

And Yorke sat at his desk, head in his hands.

He was silent for an hour or two, and then he said, 'the main problem is, I have become oppressed by other people's ideas about reality. Is this not the problem?'

Then an hour later, he said, 'Is that really the main problem? Or an offshoot of the truly main problem, which is so enormous I haven't even begun to comprehend it yet?'

He wasn't sure. He couldn't even arrive at any certainty about the nature of the problem, so how, but how, could he possibly solve it? He lacked any perspective on his own life; how could he possibly gain a perspective on anyone else's? More absurd still, lacking any perspective on anything, how could he possibly write other people's lives into a novel . . . A novel?

What the hell is a novel anyway? he thought.

A disturbing turn of events, for a novelist. Best to answer the question straight away, answer it firmly and precisely, that's that, all over, before it gets out of hand . . .

What is the novel? *Yes of course, fair enough, let's just get this absolutely clear, right now: 80,000–100,000 words (or more, or less), prose, presentation of life of*

7

characters, requiring story, plot, tension, drama. Or not.

Requiring language.

Yes! Surely!

Anthony was aware the situation was really quite perilous . . . Any further fragmentation of his sense of solidity and he would be –

Where?

Of course, he didn't know the answer to that question either . . .

II

How might we help Anthony Yorke?

Perhaps you might say, well, who cares about the dilemmas of a novelist! A member of a dubious consortium of liars, charlatans, illusionists?! Yet, the dilemma of realism and reality does not merely afflict the plaintive little novelist; it is a feature of life in general. If we are to live in reality, at all, if we are to be 'real' to others and to ourselves, then it is important that we understand what Reality is. Equally, if we are to deviate from Reality, to refuse its parsimonious allocations, then it helps, again, if we know from what we diverge. In life, in general, we are constantly assailed by notions of reality and realism, advised to 'get real,' or 'be realistic,' to measure our expectations in line with some general notion of what is real and reasonable. Yet, it is hard to determine what is real, perpetually. Theories of reality wax and wane, and one era's categorical reality is another era's outmoded supposition. A person who is real and present today might well, due to the uncanny conditions of mortality, and the finitude attached to everything, become abruptly unreal and absent. History is scattered with lost realities, discarded precepts. The grand enterprises of philosophy, science, theology and general experience in the world require us, nonetheless, to reiterate this unanswerable question, over and over, like so many Sisyphuses toiling up mountains crying as we labour: 'What is reality?'

Who determines what is real and unreal? Who is the judge?

Anthony Yorke has perhaps been a little cast down by these questions. He is not omniscient, so he does not know, eternally and truthfully, what Reality is anyway. So he does not know when he is adhering to the precepts of Reality, and when he is not. He feels that his work and perhaps his own life is not convincing, not truthful; or, worse besides, he has no idea how he could judge such things, how he might ascertain whether he is, at any given moment, being truthful or mendacious, right or wrong.

Yet, help is at hand! As I sit and type these words, I am at a computer. This is, in itself, a sort of reality: the glittering elsewhere of the screen, a realm in which we are present and yet immaterial. Furthermore, my fascinating computer has a theory of reality. It even sounds blissfully certain of this definition and indeed of the factual properties of language. My computer tells me:

REALITY –
– The world or the state of things as they actually exist, as opposed to an idealistic or notional idea of them: **he refuses to face reality | Laura was losing touch with reality.**
– A thing that is actually experienced or seen, esp. when this is grim or problematic: *the harsh* **realities of** *life in a farming community | the law ignores* **the reality of** *the situation.*
– A thing that exists in fact, having previously only existed in one's mind: *the paperless office may yet become a reality.*
– The quality of being lifelike or resembling an original: *the reality of Marryat's detail.*

Thus, my computer explains, Reality is *things as they actually exist*, as opposed to *idealistic* or *notional* ideas of them. Reality is things as they exist *in fact*, rather than *in one's mind*. This all sounds distinctly reassuring. There are facts, and actualities, and these are real. Then, on the other side, there is 'one's mind,' in which things are not real. Anthony Yorke is concerned that his character is not real. Well, we might say: your fears are quite justified! Your character exists solely in your mind and, therefore, according to a computer-dictionary, she is totally unreal. Non-factual! Absurd novelist! And yet, equally, Yorke is concerned that nothing, at all, is quite real, that everything is subject to flux, that established certainties may fade and that even the parameters of general reality, the way he is told to comprehend the solid and ostensibly material world, may change. For, after all, what are Things anyway? Are they entities, or atoms, or particles, or something else entirely? Are they tangible aspects that we can see, or nanoparticles we cannot? Are things not defined in different ways, in given eras: the humours, the ether, dark matter, the stratosphere?

What does it mean, furthermore, for things to be as they *actually* are? Where is the dividing line, between the apparent and the non-apparent, the real and the non-real, the thing and the non-thing? In order for there to be Things as they Actually Are, one assumes there must be Things as they Actually are Not, or at least, Things that do not quite qualify as Actual, and exist in a shady hinterland of the not-quite-real Real.

We might aim at rigour, and devise a list of the Actual versus the Notional:

Actual	*Notional*
Real Life	Fiction
Physical Pain	The notion of pain
War	The notion of war
Language?	Or should language be over here – Language

Yet, surely language only exists in the mind? Not actually at all?

Yet: language summons actualities: first the notion, then the thing?

Or: language denotes actualities; that is, represents reality?

Which comes first, the word or the thing? *Logos*, or the world?

If language, emanating from the mind, is merely notional, not actual, then perhaps nothing we say is real at all, according to the computer's definition of reality – and so our parameters – actual versus notional – have ceased to exist.

Yet, we must preserve ourselves from the abyss, lest we fall into nonsense, the madness of unmeaning. There are things around us – actual things – as the computer has advised. They are real. The sun will rise each day and set each evening. We do not know that the sun has always done this, we do not know it always will, or rather our science tells us that the sun, in actual fact, will not always rise, and one day will vanish, but this is not quite relevant to the reality of our contemporary epoch. Insofar as we all experience Reality, the Sun will rise each day and set each evening.

We also know that death is real, that it is objectively true that we will all die, and our parents will die if they have not already, and everyone we love must die, and we do not want to consider any of this. There are times you do not want to accept this is Real. And it is not, in a sense Real anyway.

The most insane reality of all!

Yet, we do not know what death is. In a sense?

Experientially we do not know. Or, it is a realm in which experience ceases, for the individual. And therefore, it is not real, in terms of the subjective experience of the individual self.

To this self, perhaps, death is nothing!

Therefore?

We might move on from such imponderables and depend instead on a commonsense theory of reality: that if something is generally held to be real then we might accept that this is sufficient and reasonable. Gravity, or Darwinian evolution theory, or the current prevailing theory of the Big Bang. We exist within General Reality and thus we understand that our mental processes derive from neurones and our hearts pump blood around our bodies and such collective suppositions about the world are dependable and yet –

Alas –

This is not coherent at all.

If many people agree with a vile and genocidal regime, that does not make the regime objectively correct, of course. If a group of people believes itself to be superior to those of a different race or nationality or religion, it does not mean they are objectively right. Reiterations of the same gross leaden moronism do not render them 'factual' and 'real'. The general reality of one era may be the lunacy of the next. No one worships Osiris, Inanna, Zeus, Mithras. No one muses on the probable existence of the ether. If I am feeling ill, my doctor will not tussle me to the surgery floor and apply leeches. Such realities, once authoritative, are now vanquished.

To roll over again, on the cold frosted ground, or the surgery floor, and reverse everything, we might also consider an opposing strand of thought. Plato argued that the most real Realities are in fact the things we cannot see. The invisible is the Real and the Visible is the Unreal. Plato presented the Dividing Line, a diagram which indicates the transition between the visible and the invisible realms, with the invisible realm knowable only through the mind. A similar notion informs the mystical idea of Maya – that material reality is an illusion – and countless pantheons of invisible deities, throughout time. Gods and goddesses. Demons and angels. Heaven and Hell.

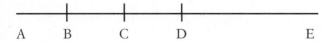

Yet, the question remains: how does Plato know? If you quest for adamantine meaning, then you arrive, perhaps, not at a line but at a spiral, which swirls around and around the same unresolvable question: how might we judge what is real, from within the dilemma, and not beyond it? To create an absolute, objective Dividing Line would require you to transcend the parameters of reality; to become something beyond human. To become eternal, omniscient and therefore unreal.

This is evidently a major paradox.

III

Deep in this paradox, Anthony Yorke sat, day after day, then for a week, he sat, he wrote, he deleted everything, he failed indoors and outdoors, he began again –

Unrealities swirled around him, and he could not lasso anything that appeared to be remotely tangible – or Real.

Time passed . . .

He thought . . .

Yet the precepts of the mind are unreal, and thus – it seemed futile to think at all –

Or, they are absolutely Real, and nothing else is Real at all –

Or, everything is impossible, unknowable – beyond comparison and redemption –

Beyond words!

Nonetheless, in the midst of this dilemma, mired in uncertainty, Yorke wrote –

Nonetheless, despite everything, he wrote:

She moved across the grass, carrying her carrying her fan and her carrying her muffler

Her hair in a chignon

Carrying a shotgun

NO

She moved on . . . The universe ebbed and flowed around her. The ether whirled around her . . .

She moved across the lawn carrying her skirt, carrying her canary, carrying her will-to-continue in the palm of her hand –

Carrying her soul in a handbag –

Carrying the world in a grain of sand –

She moved, oh how she moved, she danced and sang and emanated surreal joy across the lawn –

Oh

Woman without a name moved without a purpose across the grass without a context and she moved . . .

She moved across the grass carrying the future of humanity and the mystery of things in a small metal box . . .

This went on for a long time . . . Yorke was adrift but he wasn't even sure if that mattered; if it was an anomaly he must correct or simply a reasonable response to indeterminacy in general. Weeks of this and then these walks which failed to restore and if anything confused further and then these conversations round and round with his students (yes, Anthony was also a tutor) as they said:

But surely it doesn't matter if the omniscient narrator is a convention, it just is a convention, so, I mean, why can't we just use the available conventions? Why does every generation have to like innovate and can you even innovate within the form of the novel . . . ?

Yes, said Anthony. *You can.*

He hoped that was true.

But Professor Moore said the novel is a crude bourgeois form, and you should just accept that, it does what it does, and well, it's fine.

A young student called Nick Wilson, so lovely, so aggravating.

Really, said Anthony. *Well, you don't have to listen to Professor Moore. You don't have to listen to me either.*

Well, listen, but then go your own way. Do your own thing. Be brave! Be bold and daring!

Unlike me, he thought. Then dismissed the thought. Self-loathing, so futile. So self-regarding, even to loathe the self. Best to ignore the self, as much as you can.

The Self = Unreal Too (Anthony assumed . . .)

Ah, Yorke said to his students. *Time's up!*

But then – one afternoon –

Yorke was teetering on the brink of the abyss, looking deep deep down –

And –

Whether some craggy old divinity took pity on Yorke or whether some chance occurrence switched on something in his mind/membranes/neurones/conductors –

His internal thought-generator generated a really big thought –

The homunculus pounding on his skull . . . Wake up, Yorke, wake up . . . !

Yorke one day, in an antiseptic room, the sound of birds beyond the window –

Yorke one day

Woke – leapt to his feet –

Ragged-looking man –

And said –

Oh.

He went into the garden by the river . . . The sun was in his eyes, he squinted, saw the woman was on the grass, still walking, her thoughts still unknowable –

He didn't mind. It didn't matter so much now.

He was walking behind her, towards the house, the sound of the wind in the trees around him. Birds were wheeling in the sky, flying from the eaves of the house . . . back again . . .

The sound of water lapping the banks and a rat plashing into the river but it didn't matter now – none of it mattered –

He was walking with a gun in his hand –

A noise – a cry – came from his mouth and the woman turned–

Who are you? she said. She didn't like him from the start. Something about him unnerved her –

Well, it was probably the fact he was stalking her with a gun . . .

He said, *Sorry if I made you jump.*

Don't be sorry, she said, her voice trembling a little. *Just tell me what you are doing in my garden.*

Beautiful mouth, a bit of a cliché, a bit of a rosebud, he'd never been good at describing people in The Past, it had been his worst idea yet, to write a historical novel, but his editor had told him he should, but still – what a fool he had been –

Why won't you answer? said the woman. *I think you are very rude –*

So he aimed his gun – she screamed, put up a hand – *But, what is this? What are you doing?*

You simply don't work, he said. *I'm very sorry. I could spend another year finding out all the ways in which you simply don't work but I think it should end now.*

End? No no, she was saying. *Be reasonable . . .*

She had stopped moving, he was about to lower his gun but then he realised –

He still couldn't see her face –

Sorry, he said. *You just don't work.*

That made her weep a little, as she pleaded – *I might not work now, but I can work, I promise I'll work in the end. I'll be fine.*

He clicked the thing on the gun, noting as he did that it was a pretty sorry state of affairs when he couldn't even accurately describe a gun.

Alright, alright, she said, still pleading, despite the clear evidence of his debilitating incompetence. *Don't shoot me. I'll go, I'll just go and do something else. Just let me go, don't actually kill me.*

Well . . . he said. It was true, he had to concede. The whole stalking his characters thing, even this incursion was derivative! *But then, I might find you in some file on my computer, start wasting my time trying to write you again.*

I promise I won't. Anyway, if you see me, just ignore me. I'm off.

She was wringing some bit of her swishy dress, that cursed swishy dress – it was hard to resist the urge to blow her across the unreal grass, he didn't care, he'd call it an allusion, much better, indebtedness to the greats, he had his finger ready on the trigger, on the Trash Everything button, Trash

Don't put me in Trash, she said. *Please . . . please . . . don't . . .*

Oh Christ, alright, he said. *Just go then, Go –*

She didn't say anything else, she just picked up her skirt and ran – ran across the garden thinking whatever she was thinking and he waited on the grass with soot flecks falling on his face until she vanished into the trees . . .

IV

Having banished his unreal creation, what should Yorke do? Should he retrain, become a doctor, a lawyer, an accountant? Should he do something 'useful', abandon the lunatic quest? Freud wrote that 'Illusions commend themselves to us because they save us pain and allow us to enjoy pleasure instead. We must therefore accept it without complaint when they sometimes collide with a bit of reality against which they are dashed to pieces.' So, Yorke can hardly complain, that his childish illusions, his fantasies, have been obliterated by harsh reality. He must ascend, from the liminal realm of the imagination, into the waking world of quotidian normality, where everything must be factual, real and certain.

He might aspire to this state. He really might! And yet, what is this state? Still, he doesn't know. His unreal world has been obliterated, on the grounds of unreality; yet, what might take its place? Friedrich Nietzsche argued that 'there are no facts, only interpretations'. Freud proposes an unyielding Reality – hard, heavy, crushing our illusions. Yet Nietzsche consigns us to the realm, instead, of pure experience. There are no facts – autobiographical or material – only interpretations.

There is no judge.

Each person's experience is her own. No one else can break into it and see reality in the same way. I may know what Reality looks like to me, but I do not know what reality looks like to anyone else. You, also, create your own reality, and I can never see this version of reality as you see it. There is no fixed reality, or none that is meaningful, because each one of us disagrees about the nature of reality and therefore, to all intents and purposes, there is no Real Reality. There is just an infinite number of Realities. Each person is completely alone in Reality, trapped in solipsism and doomed to the deep aphasia of Anthony Yorke – futility, vacancy – abandonment!

Unless?

Experience is empirical data, as William James wrote.

Unless!
    Uncanny and beautiful, a wild dream –
    The reckoning of one mortal with the world –
communicated through a system of strange murmurs
– in words – or images – or music –

Then, perhaps, and even more strange, these forms –
imperilled, fragile – might resonate across ages, even
beyond the boundaries of mortal life – somehow –

So we find – Virginia Woolf, refusing the 'reality' of
others. 1923, and she refuses. She says that others may
see the railway carriage in a certain way. In the railway
carriage, she imagines, is a Mrs Brown – an exhausted,
tearful, elderly woman, being spoken to – harshly –
by a younger man. Woolf imagines other authors –
Arnold Bennett, John Galsworthy, H. G. Wells – in
this carriage, relaying their impressions. Each version
of the carriage is wildly different. Arnold Bennett tells
Woolf that her version of the carriage, of Reality, is not
real. Woolf's response is a grand assertion of dynamic
subjectivity: who are you, Arnold Bennett, to tell me
what is real? 'What is reality? . . . A character may be
real to Mr. Bennett and quite unreal to me.'
    Who are the judges of reality?
So we find: Pablo Picasso (berated for his unreal portraits, his 'distortions') asking: 'What is a face, really?

Its own photo? Its make-up? Or is it a face as painted by such or such painter? That which is in front? Inside? Behind? And the rest? Doesn't everyone look at himself in his own particular way? Deformations simply do not exist.' In so far as Picasso experiences the face, it is inverted, or supposedly distorted, except, as he says, there's no such thing as distortion or deformity.

So, we find Paul Cézanne, perceiving the shimmering contours of a tree-lined mountain as patterns of colour, and then all the gaps, the whiteness, the blankness that we see between objects, the moments when things are not quite connected and we wonder if the edifice might collapse entirely. Cézanne is painting in this way because he sees reality in this way and yet – his paintings are rejected by every artistic authority around. They are simply bad, these denizens of certainty explain. They are not true. Unreal! And then, people start sending him letters. It sounds unimaginably odd, but they actually write to admonish him (I paraphrase):

> *Dear Mr Cézanne,*
> *Your paintings are a disgrace. I hate them. I hate you.*
> *Get out of town.*
> *Yours,*
> *Upstanding Denizen of Reality and Truth*

So, we find Galilei Galileo recanting all his beliefs,

on pain of death, even though (it turns out) they are now the basis of our contemporary theories of the universe.

We find countless wise women – terrorised, beaten, burnt –

'Truth, as any dictionary will tell you, is a property of certain of our ideas. It means their "agreement," as falsity means their disagreement, with "reality."'
– William James.

This projects us into an interpretation of 'Reality' as a coercive system of ideas, which are imposed on us, whether we like it or not. We are handed a series of masks, as we progress through life, and at each stage, we are encouraged to perceive these as Real. We all live in negotiation with this wider Reality, as William James explains. We live in agreement, or disagreement with so many protocols. We are inducted into language and wider society: we are taught, steadily, to censor our thoughts, which occur to us in this learned language, strangest of all. We are told to 'be' a woman, or a man, to 'be' a child, or a parent. To conform, correctly and realistically, to these roles. We are advised to apply strictures to what we convey to the world, how we relay our finite impressions of the stuff around us: 'Things'! Certain regimes tell their populations that *There is One Reality – Ours – and no Other.* Monologues, ideological tyrants, pedal their single versions of REALITY, bolstered, ostensibly, by adamantine facts, which cannot be countered. Steadily, unique mortals are encouraged to discard their own unique perceptions of reality and accept a single immutable version – an 'unpleasant noise,' as Enrique Vila-Matas defines it.

How to escape?

'I am not Dead, I am in Herne Bay'

So wrote Marcel Duchamp in a postcard to his friend Max Bergmann at the beginning of August 1913. Duchamp was in Herne Bay to accompany his younger sister Yvonne, who was learning English. While in Herne Bay Duchamp wrote postcards and played tennis. He was greatly interested in the Grand Pier Pavilion, which had opened in Herne Bay three years earlier. Duchamp attached a postcard (by Fred C. Palmer) of this pavilion to his notes and added: 'An electric fête recalling the decorative lighting of Magic City or Luna Park, or the Pier Pavilion at Herne Bay . . . The picture will be executed on two large sheets of glass about 1m 30 x 1,40/ one above the other.' The Grand Pier Pavillion (illuminated by both gas and newly installed electric lighting) was clearly visible from the top of the downs, where Duchamp and his sister were staying. The lights would have been reflected in the ocean, to extraordinary effect.

The Bride Stripped Bare by Her Bachelors, Even (*La mariée mise à nu par ses célibataires, même*), most often called *The Large Glass* (*Le Grand Verre*), is over nine feet (2.75 metres) tall, and freestanding. Duchamp worked on the piece from 1915 to 1923, creating two panes of glass with materials such as lead foil, fuse wire, and dust. The lower panel contains the bachelors, who are suits, taken from a men's magazine. The object-machine that seems to rotate on the right could be a chocolate grinder.

In the upper panel is the Bride: three empty chambers.

The key question is: how can the bachelors reach the bride? They seem to be trapped in the lower panel. They are trapped in a machine. In a reality. They are encased in something immutable – the material realm; its rules and certainties.

If this interpretation is feasible then the bodies in each panel, the 'bride' and her 'bachelors,' will never collide.

If this interpretation is feasible then the artist, or writer, is not an arbiter of realism or reality. They do not decide what is real and true and what is unreal and false. They are bound by physical realities and powerless, in the end. To transcend reality, we have discussed already, you would need to be omniscient, immortal, trans-human, to stand beyond the parameters of all this equivocation and uncertainty and relative knowledge and total lack of knowledge and to pronounce indelibly and correctly on the meaning of all things. Therefore, you would be transhuman and translanguage and trans our understanding. The judge is effectively non-existent because they cannot exist, in this world. Yet the non-existence of the non-human judge posits another possibility: the artist's reality is the only reality, in the work they have created. Subjective experience is real. Imaginative experience is real. It is, as William James argued, empirical data – for the individual. (To hold up your own subjectivism as a general theory would be strange indeed.)

Duchamp is in Herne Bay, staring at the lights of the Pavillion reflected in the water. And then, he envisages – something – a work of his own devising. A creation. An imagined world. The bride stripped bare by her bachelors, even – an elsewhere. His own. He understands – tenuous subjective experience can be transmuted into art. The process, however, is mysterious, even alchemical. From the postcard, clipped to Duchamp's notes, from his observation of the pavilion, its scintillating lights – there emerges a gap. A seismic, beautiful and mysterious gap. A significant silence. Any art that divests itself of the meaningless parameters of the real and unreal, the truth and false, might ascend beyond such fixed empty binaries, into the alchemical realm.

'We are discontinuous beings who perish in the midst of an incomprehensible adventure' – as Bataille wrote.

This is terrifying and beautiful at the same time.

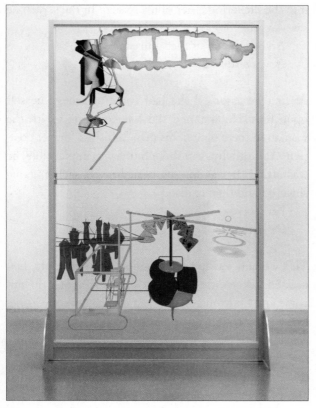

Marcel Duchamp, *The Bride Stripped Bare by Her Bachelors, Even*
(*La mariée mise à nu par ses célibataires, même*)

V

Oddly, Anthony Yorke was still here.

Around about here.

He wrote and breathed and eventually as he stared into the flickering ether of his screen. In the screen he saw – a reflection? A ghost?

An intimation of the future?

A woman!

At first he assumed she had come to avenge herself upon him. He assumed she was connected with the woman in the chignon, his own banished former creation. And briefly, even though this was implausible, he was afraid. It was for the best, he was saying, as he shivered and then realised –

Far worse –

Or better?

This woman was not the chignon monstrosity he had created. Of course! Your fictional creations do not come and find you and gun you down. Anthony Yorke knew, this couldn't happen in reality. It was inconceivable. He was a real person. Intensely and utterly real. He was not remotely post-real or proto-real, and therefore he failed to understand why this person had abruptly manifested herself before him.

'Who are you?' he said. He didn't like her from the start. Something about her unnerved him.

This woman was tall and pale, and she had a strange expression as if she was about to kill him. But this was impossible of course. Clearly he was in a dream where shadows were inverted and became something else. The usual sort of dream.

I'm sorry, she was saying.

He didn't like that at all.

Don't be sorry, he said, his voice trembling. *Just tell me what you're doing in my room.*

Of course I'd made him sketchy and demoralised. He had a sad mouth and I felt it was a shame he was so dour, but he emerged quite spontaneously: a realist novelist who had lost all conception of reality, the parameters of the real and true. He was also modelled, just a little, on Orwell's description of the book reviewer – an essay I've always loved, in which Orwell describes the professional reviewer as a prematurely aged man with appalling eyesight, who we discover slumped over his chaotic desk, a preposterous commission before him. Somehow, writes Orwell, somehow the book reviewer will prevail. Although it is logically improbable that anyone might contrive a lucid connection between five utterly dissimilar books, he will manage, somehow, to emit the requisite 500 words and even on time. Orwell's reviewer is a fervent practitioner, emboldened by desperation. This is why Yorke is male and not because I believe that the Ur-writer is male, or that the Ur-representative of humanity is male. (I hope this caveat is redundant.)

Anthony Yorke also exists in a novel I have recently written, called *A Field Guide to Reality*. In this novel he is an academic, not a novelist, and this novel is all about theories of reality and how strange they are – these adamantine or at least hopefully adamantine theories of everything. Anthony Yorke also lives in a short story I wrote last year, when my father was dying. In this story, Anthony Yorke is tormented by dreams of the departed, and eventually drawn, by these encroaching nightmares, into insanity. I only realised much later, after my father died, that this story was partly about my inability to save my father or to ameliorate his suffering. For months, before and after the death of my father, I was troubled by bad dreams and these had an intensely tactile and auditory quality, and often seeped into the ensuing day, like a miasma. In my dreams the dead were alive and particularly my father, and he was in pain in these dreams and sometimes even angry with me, as he occasionally was towards the end of his life, when his suffering was unbearable. So Anthony Yorke is somehow connected to the death of my father. He is also probably connected to the insane hopefulness of writing, of converting fragmentary, unknowable, fleeting experience into words. Yet he also derives from elements I have neither fathomed nor conveyed into conscious thoughts, I assume, which may occur to me later, or not at all.

Why are you here? said Yorke.

Why won't you answer?

What is the answer?

The realist, of course, wouldn't be here at all. The realist novelist does not insert herself into the narrative. Impossible! Imagine George Eliot adding herself to the pantheon of characters in *Middlemarch*. Or, Henry James coming onstage during *The Portrait of a Lady*, to consider the great dilemma of who, just who, dear Isabel should marry. Certain novelists devise dynamic and opinionated narrators – Jane Austen, Charles Dickens, Sigrid Undset, Doris Lessing – but these are narratorial voices, not scene-poaching manifestations of themselves. The realist author stands aloof from her creations – observing them from above, occasionally intruding into their thoughts and kindly revealing these to the reader. Thus, we perceive the minds of others in a realist novel – an unreal notion, but we are permitted this luxury, within the protocols of realistic representation.

Why are you here? said Yorke again.

Of course, the postmodernist would barely pause to answer this question. *I am here,* she would say, *because this thing you call the novel is a crazy contrivance and I can do what the hell I like! If I want to appear as myself, or if I want to appear as my dead grandmother, then that's all fine. If I want layers upon layers of novelists berating their creations, like Russian dolls, each one hopping out of an abandoned version of reality, then that's my choice. Anything goes in the ruins of civilisation!*

Why am I here? In this essay? In Anthony's room?

I am here, I said. *Because I live, also, in this formlessness.*

Anthony bridled. I understood his irritation: the remark hadn't come out as I intended.

What does, in truth?

Yet now the walls of the room, the antiseptic walls, collapsed entirely and we perceived – a great gap. In this gap was – nothingness. Darkness. From this realm in which we stood, a layering of possible realms, we discerned – another realm in which all these old certainties, old binaries, were dissolved: truth versus lies, fact versus fiction, reality versus unreality. Vanquished!

An alchemical realm, of strange worlds and words and unknown realms of experience; the mysterious nature of our selves.

So, said Anthony Yorke.

The noise echoed around the formless no longer room and drifted into the gap –

And then, surprisingly, Anthony moved. I hadn't

expected him to move, at all, but now – he stepped into the formlessness. And abruptly – he was divested of all the stymying assumptions, the weight that crushed him. And he was no longer even Anthony Yorke, a broken man, a character, in a room which might be the Large Glass or the railway carriage or just a room. He entered a sublime and improbable hoy of alterity and elsewhere and thus he was no longer he and no longer she and instead Hoy moved into a region of Light.

AY is writing – (Barbaric AY! One more allusion – we cannot escape, even here . . .)
    And Hoy remembers that Hoy is perfectly unreal, and yet here, now – just here once – for this moment –
    The invented creation of a finite mortal who is here, now – just here once –
    For this moment –
    Hoy writes –

Divested of the need to be certain, to be objective, to be 'real,' our ragged old forms – art, fiction, the 'unreal' manifestations of experience – can venture freely into this wild unknown –
    The unknowable –
    The alchemical –

This is nothing and everything, all at once –

Gabriel Josipovici

– The Work of Art –

I consider the work on the music to be such an essential
part of my life that if it were given to me to receive it
ready-made I would feel cheated.
– Igor Stravinsky

In the spring of 1985 the French newspaper *Libéra-
tion* sent a questionnaire to some of the leading
writers of the time. It consisted of just one question:
'Why do you write?' The most arresting response was
also the shortest. Samuel Beckett answered in just
three (four if you fill out the elision) monosyllables:
'*Bon qu'a ça.*' In characteristically late Beckettian manner this elicits both laughter and reflection through its
extreme concision, and, as with all Beckett's work, it
is impossible to separate anguished confession from
rhetorical bravura, with the further twist that the writing is painfully aware of the fact that the rhetoric both
reinforces and undermines the anguish. 'All I'm good
for' or 'It's the only thing I'm any good at' catches the
broad meaning but misses all that makes the phrase
memorable. (Is there also an echo there of Jean-Bédel
Bokassa, the appalling deposed head of the Central
African Republic and self-styled Emperor of Central
Africa, who had settled in France and rumours of

whose hidden and illicit wealth were rife at the time? I wouldn't put it past Beckett. I have hidden riches, he would be suggesting, but they are not really mine.)

But even the broad meaning is striking in its implicit rebuttal of the more high-flown defences of the making of art that have been common since the time of the Romantics, as well as of those who have nothing but contempt for the making of art in our modern world, whether, like Duchamp, because they recognise or think they recognise the lies and compromises on which such making is based, or because, like some recent polemicists, they wish to argue that anyone seriously concerned with understanding the world should read history or journalism or watch videos, and leave the reading of novels in particular to old ladies in rural English villages. However, most artists, whether novelists, painters or composers, whatever their public pronouncements, would probably agree with Beckett. We all go on doing what we find we can do well and drop what we can't, whether it be baking, high-board diving or playing the markets. A few, driven individuals, go on longer and with more intensity, often because they recognise that they are not much good at anything else in their lives, and this can lead to triumph or tragedy or, as with artists like Beethoven and van Gogh, to both.

Yet Beckett's memorable formulation conceals as much as it reveals. One has only to read his novels and plays, and especially his letters, to realise that in his case at least there are deeper reasons for writing, reasons so deep and so obscure that they cannot be examined except in the act of writing itself. And this is true of most artists. Specific traumatic events may spark particular works or even lead to a deepening (or, in some cases, a weakening) of the artist's oeuvre – the death of his mother in the case of Proust, exile from his beloved Russia in the case of Nabokov, the Irish troubles in the case of Yeats ('Mad Ireland hurt you into poetry', in Auden's memorable phrase). But the deeper question of why Proust, Nabokov and Yeats turned to literature and made it the centre of their lives is not addressed by this nor, in the end, by the notion that this is what, from the start, they knew they were good at.

I want to talk here about something that tends to get overlooked in discussions of art and its relation to the world, and that is the work of art, giving the word *work* as much verbal force as possible. That such work is fundamental is attested by the innumerable sketches and drafts of the mature work of Dostoevsky, Yeats, Proust and many others which have come down to us. Discussion of these usually gets relegated to the ends of introductions to canonical works – *Crime and Punishment*, *À la recherche du temps perdu* – and is often regarded by the general reader as of interest only to the scholar. But I confess to being fascinated by the way great writers gradually shape the material they start with into the books we know and love, and to finding the notebooks of Henry James, the diaries of Kafka, and Virginia Woolf's *A Writer's Diary* often more moving than their finished works. Nor do I think – certainly when it comes to works written after, say, 1800 – that this is a merely scholarly or pedantic interest; on the contrary, I think it often takes us to the heart of what these artists are up to, whether they are aware of it or not.

But even more important than this, it seems to me, is the fact that behind each work (noun) there is a hinterland of unbroken activity, even when, as in the cases of Kafka and Proust, the artists often suggest that they are lazy and idle. And as the remark of Stravinsky's that I have chosen as an epigraph to this essay suggests, it is highly probable that the *work* is what is important and that they would feel bereft if some benign but misguided god were to gift the works to them ready-made.

It is, then, the work that goes into the making of art I want to focus on, and I will do it in the only way I know, by talking personally. In the late nineties the German academic Monika Fludernik approached me and asked if I was willing for her to write a book on my fiction and drama. I was of course touched and flattered, but warned her that since I had difficulty getting my books published, what chance hers? She replied that she would take care of that (and did, it was published by Peter Lang in 2000), but what she needed from me was permission to look through my archive. I happily gave it and she spent a week-end at my house browsing through it. To my delight, among other things, she unearthed a story I had written at the age of thirteen and completely forgotten. It had appeared in *The Cairo Victorian*, the magazine of the English school I attended in Egypt, and I had a copy of it on my shelves. It is called 'The Road', and here it is in full:

The road winds slowly through the country. An overwhelming stillness surrounds it. The light is just done and a heavy mist hangs in the air. The road has been like this for the past fifty years: quiet, clean and beautiful.

Such little traffic passes; occasionally a man on a horse or a cart, or perhaps some noisy group of campers or hikers; but the road remains the same. It is a long road, yes, and very narrow. It is not tarred, and not very even, but though it has been repaired recently it still retains its personality.

Suddenly, on a tree, a bird twitters, a cock crows in the distance: it is the dawn. Soon the old road-mender will come to his beloved road, and painstakingly repair a few defects. It is really his road, for when it was on its way to decay he looked after it and nursed it back to health.

Oh! His beautiful road! It is fully 26 miles in length, and stretches through hills and vales all the way.

The little birds wait for the road-mender – the road waits for him; a little way down the road a farmer's horse puts his head over the hedge and neighs, for it is used to seeing the road mender at this time every day. It seems as if the very air waits for him, but he does not come.

It is noon; it is 4 o'clock; it is twilight, and the road-mender still has not come.

He will not come, for he is gravely ill. Remember, he has no-one to look after him, like the road has; he is alone and yet at peace with the world.

In many ways this is embarrassing, ill-written, naïve and sentimental. It does not quite know what it is doing. But what struck me when Monika showed it to me and still strikes me today is that, buried somewhere inside it, is the voice I associate with the best of my later writing. Partly this must be the result of the particular circumstances in which I grew up – born in France during the war, taken after the war by my mother to Egypt, where she had been born, and sent to an English school there, though at the time I spoke only French, and so feeling neither French nor Egyptian nor English nor anything else, and not inward with any language or culture or even landscape. Where had I seen such a road? Not in Egypt, certainly, and I doubt whether in Nice or La Bourboule either. No, I had conjured it out of my reading of English books and called upon it when I needed to express something about – I suspect – loneliness, the comfort of daily labour, the sense of one person caring devotedly for another as I felt my mother had cared for me in the threatening environment of a country at war and then in one whose language and culture still felt very alien to me even as a teenager. The particular tone of the story, rather different, I suspect, from what one normally finds in school magazines, has, I think, found its way into much of what I have subsequently written, suggesting that tone or voice is something we are born with or that is the product of ones' earliest years and, however formative the experiences of our teens and later life, it remains constant. I find the same strange sense of naivety and confidence in the first letters of Proust and Kafka or in their adolescent contributions to the albums of friends.

Though I went on writing throughout my teens what I subsequently wrote was a good deal less arresting than this early piece: I had become self-conscious and the tone had vanished. In 1957–8 I found myself in England with a year on my hands between school and university. We had moved to Putney and I made use of the wonderful public libraries there, devouring the works of Mann, Kafka and, finally, Proust. From Kafka's *Diaries* and from Mann and Erich Heller's wonderful book on him, *The Ironic German*, I learned that the difficulties I was encountering with my writing had existed for others besides myself; from Proust that there is no such thing as failure – if you hit a brick wall you have to incorporate the wall into the work. But there will always be a gap between what one knows and what one does. You have to discover what works for you, not for Kafka and Proust. I couldn't write like them, nor did I want to. But though I spent my mornings working on a novel (inevitably, about my childhood in Egypt), it was so bad and I had such little faith in it that I burned it as soon as it was done.

Why it was so bad when I had given it everything I had was a mystery, but there it was. In the following years, at Oxford, I wrote and published stories in University magazines, and one day an enterprising publisher (later a distinguished agent), Gillon Aitken, got in touch and asked to see more of my work. I was tremendously excited, re-read all I had so far written, and sent him all I felt I could stand by. However, it turned out he was only interested in a novel. I said I didn't have one but would naturally send him anything I did manage to write. A friend of mine who had been the subject of a similar approach by another publisher promptly sat down and produced a novel. Why couldn't I?

The frustration went on through my two years of graduate work and my first two years as an Assistant Lecturer in the newly formed University of Sussex. By then I was desperate to write something longer than the short stories I was producing and which no-one seemed to want to publish. Partly this was because I longed to have something substantial to work on, something that would keep me occupied over a period of months or years rather than weeks, partly because I felt that if I didn't write a novel I couldn't consider myself a writer (I hadn't yet read Borges and Robert Walser, who might have made me think differently), and partly of course because, as Gillon Aitken had explained to me, publishers weren't interested in short stories from unknown authors. My frustration had reached such a pitch that I was even feeling that, much as I loved my work at Sussex, I would have to give it up, since I didn't want to spend the rest of my days living the comfortable life of an academic while feeling deep down that I had betrayed the most intimate part of myself out of laziness or fear or for some other unfathomable reason. But the trouble was that, much as I longed to write something extended, I found myself totally incapable of doing so. For if I devised a plot beforehand I found it so boring to flesh out that the whole business of writing suddenly seemed meaningless; while if I didn't have a plot the impetus petered out after a few pages. In my rage and despair I would sometimes get up from my chair and bang my fist against the wall until it hurt so much it drove everything else out of my mind.

Then, one day, a word came into my head: *inventory*. At once I knew something important was happening. Simply repeating the word to myself gave me gooseflesh, and I realised it was because the word seems to pull in two opposite directions at once: in the direction of absolute objectivity (an inventory list) and in that of absolute subjectivity (invention). I soon discovered that they derived from two quite different Latin words, *invenire* and *inventarium*, but that didn't matter, there they both were, nestling within that single English word. And this immediately gave me my subject: someone has died and the family, with the help of a solicitor, is making an inventory of the objects he (it soon became clear to me it had to be a he) has left behind. As they do so the objects or the situation lead each of them into a recollection, or perhaps an invention, of the person they had known and of their relationship to him. And yet, though I had my subject I still could not get the novel going. There seemed to be an insuperable barrier between whatever I sketched out in my notebooks and any actual novel.

I was looking forward to a term of paid leave at the end of my first three years at Sussex (ostensibly to write a critical book) and all through that third year I pushed myself to get my novel started, and all through that year I found I just could not do it. Spring came and then summer, and still there was nothing. A beloved cat of mine had died and I decided, to take my mind off my anxiety, to write a children's story about him. I had no children of my own but I did know and like very much a colleague's three little girls, who had been very fond of the cat. So I imagined myself telling them his story. Day after day I sat down and wrote what I heard myself telling them. He had been a large neutered Tom, already an adult when we inherited him, and when he sat out in the garden contemplating the world he resembled nothing so much as an isosceles triangle with fuzzy edges. I called my story *Mr Isosceles the King.*

The advantage of a children's story was that I had no great expectations of myself and so no inhibitions to overcome. I also had a clear audience in mind. And so I found myself, day after day, while on holiday in

Italy, writing about Mr Isosceles, until one day it was finished and I realised I had a book there which I had had no idea I would write and certainly no idea of what it would be about only a month or two previously. So, as summer turned to autumn, I had a new sense of confidence that just sitting and writing for a few hours every morning would yield something. Yet that did not allay my mounting sense of panic. I knew that if I did not manage to write my novel I would have to leave the University and I had absolutely no idea what sort of job I would be able to get to keep myself and my mother – all I knew was that it would certainly be a good deal less enjoyable than the job I had.

But fear, I discovered (I was discovering a great deal in those months) can be a very useful emotion. It can push one past all the inhibitions that have been holding one back and get across that seemingly insurmountable barrier between notebook and novel.

I had the first scene in my head: the solicitor arrives at the house and meets the family of the deceased. I could visualise the street and the house. But how to convey that in words? Now I was sitting at my desk determined to write five pages a day, as I had done with the children's story, this suddenly became a crucial issue – the issue, I realised, that had prevented me from getting the novel going in all the months I had been so desperate to start. Did I use one sentence to describe the scene? Or one paragraph? Or one page? Did I adopt a matter-of-fact tone or try to write as 'beautifully' as possible? Did I let a note of irony creep in or did I try to be chummy with my reader? As I tried out one version after another I found I was deeply unhappy with them all. None, it seemed to me, did what I wanted to do. They were all written in the voices of all the novels I had ever read, but not in mine. But what was my voice? How did I set about finding it? Did I perhaps simply have to grit my teeth and keep going in this unsatisfactory mode in the hope that it would emerge? But surely I hadn't got into the business of writing simply to grit my teeth and do something I didn't believe in. I had got into it because I obscurely felt it would release something in me that would otherwise remain blocked for ever. But how to release it? And release what exactly?

Suddenly, under pressure, the breakthrough occurred. I realised that what I actually wanted was for the characters to be talking to each other, engaging with each other and with the inventory and the dead man. And then it came to me that I didn't need to describe the road or the house. If that did not interest me why not skip it and plunge straight into them talking? And then I thought: Why not write my entire novel in a mixture of dialogue and inventory lists? At once the book became a challenge and a pleasure instead of a dutiful chore. It might be difficult, it might be almost impossible, but that made it exciting. My heart was pounding – I plunged in.

'Mr Stout?' said the woman who opened the door.

'Hyman,' said Joe. 'Mr Stout's on holiday. In Corsica.'

'Gill said it would be Mr Stout,' said the woman doubtfully.

Joe shrugged.

'They could at least have sent one of their permanent staff,' said the woman.

'I am one of their permanent staff,' said Joe.

'You look like a student,' the woman said.

'As a matter of fact,' said Joe, 'and if you want me to be quite precise, I *am* their permanent staff.'

'You'd better come in,' the woman said.

'Thank you,' said Joe.

'I'll lead,' said the woman. 'Close the door behind you and give it a push or it won't stay shut.'

'I'm afraid,' he said to the woman, 'I stepped on something which gave a kind of squeak.'

'What kind of squeak?'

'Well, sort of high-pitched I suppose.'

'Don't worry,' she said. 'That was probably one of Mick's toys. He leaves them about everywhere. I hope you broke it.'

'I rather think I felt it move,' he said.

'Some of them even do that,' she said. 'But it may have been Oscar.'

'It felt more like Oscar,' he confessed.

Years later I read a remark of Duchamp's which caught my feeling exactly: 'The question of painting in a background is degrading to the painter,' he wrote. 'The thing you want to express is not in the background.' That was exactly right. Trying to describe the road and the house had felt *degrading*. What I wanted to express was elsewhere.

I had also discovered as I worked on *The Inventory* that it is possible to set up the rhythm of the work by juxtaposing sharply differentiated scenes and having no truck with transitions. I was listening to a lot of Stravinsky at the time and I loved the way he worked with small cells, often repeated, sharp breaks and clean lines, ignoring the long Western musical tradition of development, and I found that it was possible to do the same sort of thing with fiction. And so pleasing was all this to me that I wrote my next two novels in much the same way. But by the time I had finished the third, *The Present*, I felt that something had to change. The dialogue form no longer satisfied me.

At one level things were going well. I felt more at ease in my teaching role at Sussex now it was accepted by colleagues and students that part of my time would be devoted to writing. I had had a few plays publicly performed and had started writing for radio. Yet in personal terms the years 1972–5 were very difficult for me. Our beloved collie dog had developed epilepsy in a very violent form (*grand mal* rather than the more normal *petit mal*), with fits lasting sometimes as long as thirty-six hours. I recall how we were constantly on the alert for any unusual sound which would indicate that he had fallen down somewhere in the house as a fit overtook him. I recall the six-hour sleeping shifts we took, relaying each other in tending to him, taking him round the block, woozy from his fit, so that he could relieve himself as he came out of one attack, often in deserted streets, eery under the yellow street lighting, in the middle of the night. Most of all I recall, even today, the look in his eyes when, lying beside me on the sofa as he sometimes did when I was reading, he would suddenly feel the first tremors running through his body. A human being at least is aware of the nature of his illness, but for him each terrifying fit was the first, and I could not get out of my head that look of terror and the mute appeal to me which I was helpless to do anything about, when he felt the first stirrings of that alien monster which was about to seize hold of him. Eventually, after we had tried everything, including putting him on human anti-convulsants, he had a particularly violent fit which seemed to go on and on, endlessly, and, very reluctantly, we decided, for his sake and ours, to have him put down.

At about the same time a dear friend, the gifted young poet Robin Lee, who had a history of suicide attempts, finally succeeded in taking his own life. Though he had often assured me that such episodes were well behind him, and though he and I had been at one in our dislike of Al Alvarez's then fashionable romanticising of the concept of suicide, he had once, worryingly, told me that for him suicide was like a beautiful vase in the middle of a room round which the proud owner repeatedly walks, always careful not to touch it, until one day, inadvertently or perhaps wilfully, he does so and it falls and shatters. And one day in the spring of 1975 this did indeed happen.

On top of these two tragedies, or perhaps stimulated by the atmosphere building up around me in the run-up to them, I found myself behaving appallingly to a number of people who were very close to me, causing misery and mayhem. In those months I often felt that all I wanted to do was bang my head against the wall and scream.

In these circumstances the lightness and humour, the clean lines and sharp angles of my early novels did not seem to be of any help. I have recently been looking through the notebooks I have been keeping since I first came to England in 1956. Already in November 1972 I find myself writing: 'Rhythm of slow coils. Coiling slowly round and round, swelling, growing, returning . . .' And again: 'Stopping is death. The death of the organism.' A few days later: 'Slow coils. Metamorphosis . . .' I try something out: 'And again. Returning again.' And comment: 'Not a person (subject) saying/thinking, etc (that is why it is so difficult to do.) But the words, the fiction, looking for a person, a situation . . .' At the end of that year: 'Last night. The feeling: I am all stone. All wood. No interior. Nothing to feel or think with. And the thought: this complements that other feeling of rats in a hollow body.' And: 'I have a vision of a work like a snake, forming its own articulations – the excitement or tension comes not from what it says (the story) but from what it *does*.' In March of the following year

I am reading the French psychoanalyst André Green and going to a lecture of his at the ICA: 'The work of art starts from a wound, a loss,' I record him as saying then. 'It starts from that which is not-phrase and which no phrase can accommodate and it moves towards the bursting of all phrases.' And I copy out an extract from a *TLS* review of a new book of his:

There is a discourse of the unconscious, but it is a polyphony, a polygraphy, made up of heterogeneous signifiers . . . Psychic traces of certain kinds, states of the body and actions . . . The hysteric is seen not so much speaking with his body as trapped in the speech of the body and unable to regain any fluidity.

Finally, in August 1973: 'I feel that after *The Present* I want to write a much denser novel, which keeps much closer to the centre of myself.'

But what was this centre? How did I get closer to myself? What was the self to which I felt I had to get closer? When I tried to think about these things I realised that while most people had a homeland, even if they were separated from it, a clan, even if it was dispersed, a maternal language through the filter of which all other languages would be passed, I had none of those things. My clan was my mother, who had saved us from occupied France during the war and then made the courageous decision to leave everything behind in Egypt to allow me to pursue my education in England; my country was not France, where I had been born; not Egypt, where my parents had been born and where I had spent ten years between the ages of five and fifteen; and certainly not England to which I had come at fifteen and which had provided me with a wonderful education and an exciting and worthwhile job, but which felt more and more strange and alien to me the longer I lived there. And as for language, though French was what I spoke for the first five years of my life it was bound up with the anxiety that I am sure could not help seeping into a child as we lived from day to day, waiting to see which way the war would go and whether or not we would emerge alive. It was never 'mine' as it had been Racine's and Balzac's and even Proust's. English? I even dreamt in English now, but I knew I would never have the inwardness with the language and the culture which I so loved in Dickens, in Waugh, in Muriel Spark.

But then I began to think: Perhaps this is what being a *perfect* migrant is? Someone with no attachment to place or language who knows only that what he *is* is a being on the move. And I began to wonder if this was not perhaps more typical of the human condition than our culture (any culture?) was willing to recognise. Certainly the work of Green and of Deleuze and Guattari seemed to suggest as much. The latter had just published *Anti-Oedipe,* with its suggestion that we should replace the notion of rootedness with the notion of the rhizome, the many-rooted plant, and that chimed with my notion of migration. Perhaps, I felt, I should draw strength from my very weaknesses and try and follow where my instinct was leading me, however obscure the path. (Today, of course, such questions are inescapable, but not in the seemingly stable 1970s, before the fall of the Berlin Wall and long before the disastrous wars of the Middle East, the failure of post-colonial African states to provide for their people, and climate change had propelled migration to the fore-front of our consciousness.)

Two images had come into my mind under the pressure of trying to find a form for my confused feelings of pain, loss and confusion. One was a Francis Bacon painting of a man vomiting into a lavatory, bent double over it, which I might have seen at the Tate, for it forms part of Bacon's triptych in memory of his lover George Dyer which the Tate had purchased in 1972. The other was Epstein's great sculpture of Lazarus rising and shedding the shrouds wrapped round his body, which I had discovered in the antechapel of New College when I was a student down the road at St. Edmund Hall, and which I would often drop in to contemplate in my time at Oxford. I was also listening to a lot of the music of Peter Maxwell Davies and Harrison Birtwistle, at the time far from the establishment figures they have since become but the Young Turks of British music. After the comic and parodic work Maxwell Davies had written for the Pierrot Players and the Fires of London in the 60s, he had moved to Orkney and begun to produce extraordinary, slow, intense pieces, such as *Image, Reflection, Shadow* and *Ave Maris Stella*, which drew on his work with medieval and Renaissance musical processes first expressed in his enormous works of earlier years, *Worldes Blis* and the *Second Taverner Fantasia*. These seemed to me to encapsulate much of what I was feeling my way towards in my writing.

And then I heard Birtwistle's *The Triumph of Time*. I had taken the train up from Sussex to hear it in the Festival Hall, and I remember the concert began with a Mozart symphony which I just couldn't seem to settle down to listen to at all. I was too far away from the stage. I was tired after a day's teaching. I was just not in the mood. Why, I wondered, had I bothered to come? And then *The Triumph of Time* started and I knew that I had to write my book. It knocked me backwards, that long slow ritual on strings and percussion punctuated by the piercing beautiful descant of the clarinet. Towards the end of the huge single-movement work there is the glimpse of something found, and then that too is swallowed up in the inexorable march of time. Yet, when the piece is done, it remains there as a sort of half-memory.

The piece said so much to me, spoke to me so much of what I had been thinking about and trying to put into words in my notebooks that it seemed almost a miracle that someone other than I should have written it, and gave me the feeling that I too had to, and could, find *my* way of saying these things.

When one is actively involved in a work it acts like a magnet to metal filings – all sorts of surprising things suddenly enter its orbit. Though I had ended up teaching English literature, it was the fact that it could be taught in a School of European Studies that had attracted me to Sussex. For from the start of my time in England I had felt that if I was different from the English it was because of my European connections. But recently I had begun to sense that even with my Europe-orientated friends there was something that made me different. My book of short stories and plays, *Mobius the Stripper*, had recently been awarded the Somerset Maugham Prize, an award to encourage young writers to travel, and though the prize was subsequently taken away from me on a formality (I had not been born with a British passport), the University, which had granted me a term's leave, generously extended that to a paid sabbatical. I decided to return to Egypt, which my mother and I had left twenty years previously. That visit made it clear to me that there was a Levantine and a Jewish aspect to my life which had nothing to do with Europe. I must have started thinking about this a bit earlier, for a friend and I had recently started a course at Sussex on The Bible and English Literature, and I had been learning biblical Hebrew and reading the Bible quite intensively, both in preparation for the course and out of some obscure sense that this was not some cultural monument I should engage with and not exactly a religious tract but in a sense the story of my uncles and aunts. One day I came across this phrase in the prophet Micah: 'Arise and go, for this is not your rest.' (2.10) I loved the sound of the Hebrew: *k'mu velechu ki lo zot hamenuchah*. I was excited to discover that the word for 'rest', *menuchah*, is also to be found in other places in the Bible, notably when the dove is sent out of the ark by Noah but can find no rest for her feet because the earth is still under water, and in the Book of Ruth, where it is synonymous with marriage. More importantly, I noted that that phrase, 'Arise and go' is almost identical to the one God speaks to Abram (not yet Abraham), at the start of Genesis 12: 'Go forth (*lech lecha*) from your native land and from your father's house to the land that I will show you,' and which sets him and the Hebrew people on their path away from the comfortable life amidst the irrigated fields of Mesopotamia and on to the fraught nomadism of the subsequent centuries. Indeed, the Hebrew Bible can be said to have two centres, which pull in rather different directions: the centre, if one can call it that (Deleuze and Guattari's rhizome might be a better description), of Wandering in the Wilderness and the centre of the Heavenly City, associated with Jerusalem, whether actual or ideal. At different periods in the history of both Judaism and Christianity, different groups have stressed one more than the other, but I have never had any doubts about where my own allegiance lies, or rather, which I can relate to. I lack the apocalyptic imagination to make a reality of the Heavenly City but can identify totally with the Wandering. One of the reasons I found the Bible so central to my own concerns when I began to read and think about it seriously was that there, in this ancient document, in this extraordinary body of stories which together make up one story, was a profound exploration of the difficulties and dangers, as well as of the necessity, of the migratory experience, and a profound questioning of such notions as the individual and the nation state. (I loved the fact that when Moses presses God to tell him his name He merely answers 'I am that I am' *ehyeh asher ehyeh*, which in the Hebrew is more like 'I will be because I will be', while the lack of plosives and fricatives reinforces the notion of 'being' as breath as well as process.)

As soon as I read the Micah passage, 'Arise and go, for this is not your rest', I knew I had found the epigraph for my novel, a phrase which would link my book both to my own life and to the larger life of the Jewish people, and, through them, of all mankind. After much internal debate I decided to leave the quote in Hebrew, partly because the letters looked so beautiful, but in the main to give a sense of the strangeness and otherness, the deep incommunicability of what was being said. And since Bibles are easily available and the system of reference standard it seemed to me that the interested reader had simply to look it up in English while those too lazy or relaxed to do so could just contemplate it in the alien script.

I had been going up and down the road that leads from Brixton to New Cross, a road that filled me with horror every time I entered it, so endless, so run-down and desperate was it (it must, like all of London, have changed dramatically in the forty years since I was there but I have had no desire to return), and I took that as my location. I hoped that by facing that horror, the despair of the man in Bacon's sealed room vomiting into the lavatory, by finding a way of writing it, I might regain a modicum of balance. I had learned from *The Inventory* and subsequent novels that there was a point at which I had to let go of my notes and simply write, but I was terrified that such an instinctive a procedure, not underpinned in this case even by so simple a plot as that which allowed the dialogues of *The Inventory* to develop, would lead to nothing more than an indigestible mess. Nevertheless, I felt I couldn't allow that to stand in my way, and I kept at it, day after day, not looking back.

And certain things did begin to emerge: the Epstein statue rather than the Bacon image became the real pivot of the piece and I found myself reading it as a metaphor for our need to unwind the swaddling-clothes which bind us tight as we go through life, even though at the end, when all of them have been shed, no resurrected body will emerge but we will find that, freed from what held it all together, we revert to the dust from which we came. Not because it was all a dream but because what life consists of is not the final emergence, free of all impediment, into the glorious light of the sun, but rather the struggle *towards* that ever-elusive goal.

Eventually my first draft was finished. A man is walking down a dim and deserted South London street at night. He is falling. He is vomiting into a washbasin in an empty room. He is talking to someone. Here is a brief segment:

The bulb hangs down in the middle of the room. It is lit, making the curtainless window appear like a black mirror in which the bulb itself is reflected. But the light is poor and seems to have difficulty reaching the walls of the big room. Even the washbasin and the bed are in shadow.

Silence flows away from him in dark rivers.

Falling backwards, in a wide arc, he stretches out his hand to grip the lamppost and encounters only air. The black sky presses on his face like a blanket.

Everything flows away from him. It flows outwards and away in dark rivers.

Yes, I felt, I definitely had *something* there. But what? There followed months of anguished work, scrutinising what I had done, subjecting it to more analysis and drawing more diagrams than I have ever done or ever wish to do again, in order to make sure it would stand up. In the course of this work I found that the pattern 9 + 1 was a recurrent one. I tweaked the text here and there so as to make this come through more clearly, and as I did so I realised what my title had to be: *Migrations* – nine letters plus one.

Wittgenstein writes in *Zettel* about two kinds of games: 'In one case we make a move in an existent game, in the other we establish the rules of the game.' That, it seems to me, succinctly summarises the difference between the work of art before and after 1800: In earlier ages the rules were given, the genres were known, and you worked within them; that is how Virgil, Dante and Pope, utterly different as they were, all worked. In modern times, starting, say, with Beethoven and Wordsworth, artists have had to invent or discover what the rules of the game are as well as play it. That is not easy. Some artists go on in the old ways, oblivious of the fact that it is no longer viable; a few embrace the new conditions with relish. Most struggle, finding some success, every now and again, amidst much failure. Certainly in *Migrations*, even more than in *The Inventory*, I had no idea what the rules of the game were. I had to discover them as I went, by trial and error. Not only that: I had to learn just what it was I was struggling to articulate: that what we need to shed – and it's not easy – is the deeply ingrained belief that clarity of vision, an Olympian position from which we can look down on the work and on our own lives, is what is required before we can get going (in our work, in our life). I learned too that the *work* of art, or of any other discipline for that matter, is itself a form of rest, but of rest as Yeats understood it, not as a chair is at rest but as a dancer, a tree or a spinning top is at rest. This is not a condition one can (I can) take away and live with once the work is done, but it is the condition of good work when the rules of this particular game are at least instinctively understood. Working on *Migrations* I found my frustration, rage and despair turning into a kind of rhythm, a satisfying (though frightening) daily activity, an activity in which I began to understand that we never fully understand anything but that the *work* of art can help us understand why this should be so. It did not transform my life, of course, but it helped me through a real period of crisis. Certainly I was a calmer, less angry and frustrated person when the book was done than I had been before.

And somewhere inside me I was happy. Happy to have achieved what I had set out to achieve, happy to have made something I had terribly wanted to make, something that had not existed before and would never have existed had it not been for me, my perseverance and all my hard work.

Benjamin Markovits

– The Real Story –

The summer after I graduated from Yale, I looked for a job playing pro basketball in Germany. This is something I've written about a lot in one way or another, including a novel, and after a while it has become hard for me to remember what actually happened and what it felt like. Even at the time, I knew that playing pro ball would give me something to write about. My vague plan at twenty-two was to be a poet, without any real sense of what that meant or how you could make a living at it. But I also wrote a couple of long letters home from Germany and from our training camp base in Slovakia, which took the form of journals, pieces of extended description – I was using the letters as an excuse to self-publish my impressions. What I mean is, I don't want to present this story as a way of showing the contrast between the innocent experience-hungry young man and the guilty older writer who exploited his own life for material. But that is what I ended up doing.

Five years after leaving Germany, I wrote a 'diary' piece about my obsession with Michael Jordan for *The London Review of Books*, which was also an account of the time I spent in the basketball minor leagues. It was my first real breakthrough as a writer – a cover story in a serious journal that was something more than a review of somebody else's book. By that point I had written several drafts of a longer memoir about my playing days, which had gotten me a meeting with a producer at the BBC and with an editor at Yellow Jersey Press, a new imprint of Random House that had been set up to publish literary sports writing. But nothing came of these meetings and that memoir has never been published. For reasons I was slowly beginning to appreciate: because nothing much happened in it. I mean, my half-year in Germany was in some ways the most vivid, unusual and traumatic period of my life, but it was also fairly uneventful. I flew to Hamburg, I got a job, I played basketball, I didn't like it, and I quit.

Eventually I abandoned the drafts and decided to turn the experience into a novel, *Playing Days*, which pretended to be a memoir and used my own name and included a number of details and episodes that were literally true. But a lot of it was also made up. I added some things and rearranged others in order to increase the sense of drama. Even so, what I had produced was the kind of novel editors describe as 'quiet'. At least, that's what my editor called it, but by now I had already published four novels with him and our relationship was strong. Faber agreed to bring out *Playing Days* almost as a favor to me and for not much money – they 'borrowed' some of the advance from another book I was contracted to write for them as a way of sweetening the deal. But my American editor was unpersuaded or less persuasive: she couldn't get her board to take on the novel. It was *too* quiet for them, and the kind of suggestion she came back to me with involved shifting the action from the German minor leagues (a world of which I had what seemed to me an interesting first-hand experience) to America and the NBA, a world I knew about only in the way most American sports fans know about it, by watching the games on TV.

What interested me about all this, or bugged me about it (aside from the obvious fact that I didn't like being rejected), is that it showed the difference between the way we actually experience something and the way we're willing to read about it in a book. I've been teaching now for about ten years and there's a line I use on students to describe what seems to me difficult about writing, especially when you first start out. Most of us think of our lives as essentially uneventful. Stuff occasionally happens, some of it very important, but we generally get through our days and weeks happily enough even when it doesn't. In fact, the big events seem like an interruption to something else that is going on. But novels are about things happening, and so when we start writing fiction there's this gap we have to bridge between the uneventfulness of our experience and the drama that we think is supposed to take place on the page.

This is why a lot of young writers, and not just young writers, kill off so many characters or turn them into alcoholics and suicides or push them into fights. Because we ask them all the time, what's at stake here, or what's the question, and tell them things like, drama is conflict. But even among more sophisticated writers you get the feeling that they're ramping up the tension. There's a kind of fiction coefficient, a multiplier that you need to apply to turn actual human experience into something dramatic enough for a story or a novel. In other words, to get something published you need to make it at least two and probably three or four or five times as interesting as the source material. Which has a distorting effect on the whole business, not just of writing but of reading, too. And this holds true even when the original experience seemed pretty dramatic at the time – like a twenty-two year old basketball-crazy kid, who had mostly failed at team sports, walking out of graduation and ending up, a few months later and a continent away, starting his first job as a professional athlete.

From what I can remember, the last few weeks before graduation were incredibly intense in a way that turned out to have almost zero connection to anything that mattered in my life to come. At the beginning of my final semester I had started going out with a German grad student. Let's call her Anke, which is the name I eventually gave her in the novel I wrote about playing basketball in Germany. She was interning at the Yale medical school and had a boyfriend back in Hamburg, although by the time Anke and I started seeing each other they had decided to take a break from their relationship while she was abroad. I genuinely don't know why she wanted to go out with me. I'd had a few girlfriends in college but was also still quite innocent sexually, too tall, over-jokey or else too serious, and arrogant or confident in many ways but not in the ways relevant to a relationship. I must have seemed to her very young. Anke was skinny, nervy, very pretty, boyish, freckled and maybe lonelier on her post-doc abroad than I had the sympathy to appreciate. We spoke German together, which was my first language (my mother is German) though I'm clumsy in it and make a lot of mistakes. My accent is native, though, and maybe *childish* is a truer description than clumsy: I always feel attracted to people I can speak German with, I feel quickly at home with them. Which might also explain what Anke responded to in me.

Our relationship, right from the beginning, was supercharged by her sense of infidelity. The guy in Hamburg had been her boyfriend for something like six years. I could never quite tell what the legal status of their relationship was: sometimes she seemed to think it was okay for us to see each other, and sometimes she seemed less sure. All of which meant that just holding my hand in a restaurant was hugely significant for her. There was an imbalance right from the beginning. I was just hanging out with a cute grad student, she was possibly putting an end to six years of her life, a life she already felt painfully removed from since to reach it she had to get on an airplane – and maybe even an airplane wouldn't bring her home to it after what she had done with me. Not that we did very much. I remember spending two hours over a plate of buffalo wings on a Tuesday night at Dakota J's (a bar that served half-price all-you-can-eat wings on Tuesdays), rubbing our fingers together under the table and staring at each other, feeling the weight of the impossibility of everything. Though what I actually felt was probably more like very sorry for her and attracted to her at the same time, and what she felt was – I don't know.

Mostly we kissed on the bed in my room (she had thin lips), or, as the weather got warmer on campus, outside, in doorways or dark corners. She didn't like holding my hand in public in daylight. We didn't have sex. There was one night I stayed over in her apartment (I remember it was over or near De Roses, a little deli in the graduate student ghetto by East Rock park – all of this seemed very grown-up to me, I was used to dorm rooms and dining halls), and we might have slept together, too, except we couldn't find a condom. I think we were both faintly relieved. This was a few weeks before graduation. Everything felt like it was coming to a head.

Meanwhile, my ordinary undergraduate life went on. I had already decided to spend the summer looking for a job playing basketball in Germany, so I lifted weights a few times a week, went running in the afternoons and played pick-up ball on the 4th-floor court of Payne Whitney gym. My hall-mate Rachel (we shared a fridge and a front door), who was also the long-term girlfriend of one of my best friends, filmed me on a quiet afternoon shooting hoops by myself on that court, driving and dunking and hitting 3s and turnarounds. I sent an edited version of this video to twenty-odd European basketball agents and club managers (you can find it on youtube). This kind of behavior tended to support the generally affectionate and occasionally exasperated view of me that my college friends had acquired over the four years – that I was somebody who didn't or wouldn't face the facts of life. I think a part of the exasperation came from their worry that I might never have to. They were studying for their LSATs or MCATs or GREs or looking for jobs at local papers or non-profits or applying for places on study-abroad programs. I was working on my jump shot – that's the kind of asshole *I* was.

The woman who first introduced me to Anke was part of a circle of friends from Pierson College (one of the residential units at Yale, which were called colleges out of a deeply ingrained sense of Oxbridge envy), and as the last few months and then weeks and days of our undergraduate lives approached, I spent more and more time with these people – including a girl called Caryn, another English major, who was also an unusually decent, sensible, lively and good-natured human being. I used to flirt with her by making up anagrams for her name. Racy Brandy and Randy by Car were two I remember. My relationship with Anke was off and on and she didn't want to get in the way of my seeing other people. I don't know if Caryn had any interest in me, but nothing happened apart from the fact that I teased her a lot to siphon off whatever sexual tension existed between us, and that we did stuff like make a mix tape of songs to take with us after graduation. She was heading to Chile, to teach English; I was flying to Hamburg. We alternated songs. One of hers was Van Morrison's 'These Dreams of You', which includes the lines 'I dreamed you paid your dues in Canada' and which I still associate with those last few odd dusty (because dorm rooms are dusty, and everybody was packing up) weeks of college life.

Part of what complicated my friendship with Caryn was that she still hung out with my ex-girlfriend, whom I had hardly spoken to since we broke up at the end of freshman year. So hanging out with Caryn also meant running into Evelyn. Unsurprisingly, I liked her less than I used to. Her general friendliness seemed to me a little sugary now, rather than simply sweet, and we weren't really very alike or interested in the same things. At the same time, I had started to realize that I must have been a fairly awkward freshman-year boyfriend for a nineteen-year-old girl. She was the first girl I ever kissed or slept with, I took the whole thing too seriously and tried to justify this new kind of intimacy by treating it as an extension of my family relationships

– I have always been very close to my family. In the long run I turned out to be grateful that she broke up with me (the short run involved extreme unhappiness), but partly because of the lack of contact since then, some of my old feeling of ungainliness around her and attraction to her had remained.

Two weeks before graduation, I drove down with a bunch of my Pierson buddies to Pauley's Island in South Carolina, where we had rented a house on the water. Caryn and Evelyn were there, too. I don't remember much about this week, except that I went jogging before breakfast along the beach – Caryn sometimes joined me. I had suffered a deep knee contusion playing basketball a few days before, which made it difficult for me to bend my leg, and I was worried about getting out of shape by the time my first try-outs in Germany came around. (This, in fact, is what happened.) Also, on the last night, somebody decided it would be a funny idea for everybody to go skinny-dipping. He was drunker than I was, which isn't saying much, because in those days I didn't drink. But I soberly took off my clothes and waded in with everybody else. I remember seeing Evelyn naked again for the first time in three years or at least topless (we were waist-deep in water, standing in the loud surf), and I tried not to act weird about it or ignore her but find the middle ground in between. Maybe I splashed her once, I don't remember, that's what people were doing, surging around and giggling and feeling cold, but years later I included this small incident in a novel, where it was meant to stand for that hard-to-untangle combination of anger and attraction which my protagonist felt for his freshman year ex-girlfriend and which I probably felt for Evelyn. It was also supposed to bring home to him the sense that he hadn't really grown up, a realization that was accompanied by feelings of sexual shame. Later, I cut the scene. It wasn't really important to the plot.

The next day we drove back to New Haven, about thirteen hours in the car. I couldn't drive at the time, I didn't have a license, another example of the kind of unworldliness that annoyed my friends. My parents and two sisters who were still living at home flew in for graduation, and at some point during that weekend I introduced Anke to my mother.

This must have been a semi-complicated meeting for her. I mean, for my mother. Her younger son, her baby boy, was about to graduate and had been dating an older woman with a boyfriend for the past few months. Not only that, Anke was German, slender and pretty, and looked probably something like my mother had looked thirty years before, when she came from Berlin to Ithaca, New York on a Fulbright scholarship and met my father, who was then an undergraduate at Cornell. This is what my mother said to me at the time, about Anke: 'I know just what she's like.' She didn't mean it in a catty way or even really in a particularly admiring way – she meant it as a fact. *I know that kind of German girl, because I used to be one of them.*

I remember thinking, I'm not so sure. The generation gap seemed significant to me. Also, Anke had been on her best behavior, which is an oddly timeless or naturally old-fashioned kind of behavior. There were things Anke had admitted to me, in the way you do when you start going out with somebody, that I found hard to square with my understanding of my mother. But maybe that says more about me than about her. I didn't know my mother when she was twenty-five years old.

The graduation ceremony was on Sunday (people were upset, because our commencement speaker was Henry Winkler, also known as the Fonz from *Happy Days*; classes before us had been addressed by presidents and famous writers), and on Saturday night a number of my Pierson friends decided to have a sleepover. At Caryn's place or Evelyn's place or somebody else's place, I don't remember – it had a largish common room where a lot of people could sleep. I had dinner with my family at Bangkok Gardens, which is what I thought of at the time as our local fancy restaurant, then went back to my room and packed up a few more things: un-blu-tacked posters from the wall and rolled them into tubes, filled cardboard boxes with books. Around ten o'clock, I pulled my mattress out of the frame and dragged and carried it down a flight of stairs, across the courtyard, and up another flight of stairs, to the sleepover. There still weren't enough beds to go around and I ended up sharing the mattress with

Caryn. She has curly hair, which tickled my face and kept me awake. Evelyn was lying on another mattress in my line of sight. I didn't sleep much. It all seemed very . . . gung-ho in a high-schoolish way, emotional or sentimental – it wasn't the sort of thing I did in college, or in high school either, for that matter. But it was pretty intense, too, drifting in and out of sleep all night with this very nice girl in your arms who you never would kiss, while this other girl who broke your heart lay a few feet away.

At some point on that Sunday afternoon I took a last walk with Anke. She made a point of holding my hand ('I should live up to what I'm really doing') and gave me as a parting gift a single condom, in its crinkly wrapper, and a Bert and Ernie bedtime book – the kind you can attach to a stroller. In it, she had written: 'for the long nights'. Fifteen years later I ended up reading that book to my kids when they were babies, just because it was lying around. The condom was a kind of promise, of her intentions towards me, or maybe it was more like a token of her feelings, because we both knew at the time that we would never get a chance to use it. That night, after the ceremony, after I threw my hat in the air with everybody else, my brother drove me to Boston, which is where he lived. And two days later I flew to Hamburg to start looking for work as a basketball player.

As a kid, we used to travel on airplanes all the time. Every summer we flew from Austin to London or Hamburg (my mother's family still has a house, about two hours from Fuhlsbüttel, on the Danish border) to escape the heat. Once my dad even made us take a day trip to Dallas/Fort Worth – we never left the airport, we got right on a plane coming back, just for the air miles. Planes seemed to me boring and uncomfortable and I associated them with a certain amount of stress. My parents were often trying to schlepp a year's worth of belongings, most of them packed by my mother in enormous cardboard boxes, back and forth from Europe, and some of their anxiety inevitably communicated itself to us. But I never felt an actual fear of flying until I found myself alone at the gate in Logan airport waiting for my plane to start boarding. Flights were stressful because of all the people involved (I'm one of five kids) and just the ordinary family tensions exacerbated by sleeplessness, junk food and confined spaces, but something about the fact that I was entirely alone, twenty-two years old, and about to get on a plane that would fly through the night and drop me on a different continent, where nobody especially loved me, freaked me out. I remember becoming uncomfortably aware of my breathing and that this was a problem that concentrating on it harder couldn't solve.

The reason I flew to Hamburg is that my uncle, my mother's brother, lived there. He was a bachelor psychoanalyst, a stylish and genial man (he had longish hair and often wore a little scarf around his neck, even indoors), who was used to his own routines and getting his own way. But he was basically very generous to me. In his student days, he had borrowed some money and bought a run-down apartment block in a shitty student part of Hamburg, which had become, in the intervening years, the fashionable artsy quarter. He lived in the penthouse flat and rented out many of the others cheaply to his friends, on the understanding, it seemed to me, that he could stop by whenever he liked, and they would entertain him and probably give him supper. He had never married (or only once, very briefly) or had kids, and these are the sorts of relationships he felt comfortable with – playing host and guest at the same time, among friends to whom he had been generous. He also ate out almost every night at a restaurant called the FilmHaus, a hipster cafe connected to some indie cinema, where the waiters knew him by name. This is where he took me on my first night in Hamburg.

I stayed with him, off and on, for about two months. In the next ten years, most of which I spent in Europe, I probably saw Anke, Caryn and Evelyn no more than two or three times each. With one exception, which I'll come to in a moment, they played no part in my life. The break I made that summer from my undergraduate existence was clean and quick.

While waiting at the gate in Logan airport, and afterwards, on the plane, before falling asleep, I started writing a poem in my head, which I had plenty of time at my uncle's place to tinker with on the page. I also wrote letters, some of them to Caryn, who had made a similar clean break and was finding her feet in Chile. On most days I woke up late and tried to stay out of my uncle's hair (I think his apartment had only one shower) before he went to work – his office or surgery may even have been on a different floor of the same block of flats. I ate out a fair amount, too, I didn't want to make his kitchen dirty. Besides which, I had never really cooked for myself. The rest of the time I jogged, shot hoops on public courts to keep my eye in, and every few days took a train somewhere, with a change of clothes and a basketball in my duffel, looking for a job – trying out for various clubs, in Hamburg itself, and Gelsenkirchen, and Würzburg, all over the country.

The refrain of this poem, which knocked around my thoughts for much of that summer, went something like this: *The 22 blues are as clear as the sky.* Which is more or less how I felt. I was lonely but it was fresh loneliness, it still smelled clean. I was drifting, the world seemed very big around me, I was getting used to the company of my own head, and there were days when I hardly spoke to anyone, which suited me fine. The weather, in fact, was terrific – hot and clear, day after day. I was young, anything could happen, and at that time my real ambition in life was to become a poet, and the work I spent scribbling away at this poem seemed just as important and pointless as the hours I put in on the mostly empty public courts of Hamburg, shooting hoops.

But as soon as I landed a job, in Landshut, a small town outside Munich, and just about as far from my family roots in Northern Germany as you could get while staying in the country, I flew to London, where my parents were spending July. I wanted to go home, or whatever was standing in for home at my parents' borrowed apartment, and pretend that none of this was happening and that I was still a kid on summer holiday, messing around until school kicked off in September.

In fact, training camp started the first week of August, and a guy called Kresimir Miksa (nicknamed Grescho), a six five herky-jerky Eastern European type with a boxer's beat-up face, picked me up from the Munich airport in the coach's car and smoked and got lost on the way to the team lunch. I wrote about much of what happened next in my novel, though I changed all the names.

I changed a few other things, too, some for obvious reasons and some less obvious. One of the stars of our league was a seventeen-year-old kid named Dirk Nowitzki, who eventually signed a twenty-five million dollar contract with the Dallas Mavericks, and won league MVP honors and finally an NBA championship about fifteen years after I knew him. I played against him several times, including a pre-season tournament in – I can't remember where it was – but it was the only time all year I started or logged significant minutes, because our point guard had pulled up short running wind sprints a few days before, and strained his hamstring. I averaged about ten points a game and Nowitzki and I guarded each other for a few brief spells. Those were the only points I scored all year, partly because I got injured (a few months later one of my teammates broke my cheekbone throwing an elbow he was aiming at somebody else) and partly because by the time I was cleared to play again I was too unhappy to want to. I was also, as it turns out, not good enough.

In the novel, I changed Dirk's name to Karl and switched him to our team, to bring him closer to the action. This put him in competition with the 'hero' of my story, a six two shooting guard named Bo Hadnot, from Mississippi, who was also, in the novel, the ex-husband of Anke and the father of her three-year-old daughter. By the time I had started writing this novel I had a daughter myself, and she made her way into the story – partly because I had realized that the occasionally intense but mostly drifty and exhausted way a young parent gets through the days mirrors pretty accurately the life of a professional athlete. Hadnot got his name from a running back for the Texas Longhorns, my hometown college football team, and was partly based on a kid I played basketball with in grad school, a big-toothed handsome tobacco-chewing southerner who liked to talk a lot and could really shoot. Dead-eye shooters have always interested me. The art of shooting seems like such a simple and transparent mechanism for the process that separates failure and success. A ball goes in or it doesn't. But nobody like Bo Hadnot played for us in Landshut.

The man he stood in for was almost too interesting a character to be plausible or useful in fiction. Johnny Roberson was the real star of our team, a skinny power forward who grew up in San Antonio, about an hour from my hometown in Austin. He had had a 'cup of coffee' in the NBA (I think he got cut by the Spurs in training camp) before bouncing around various European leagues. The year before he came to us he had played for the Sundsvall Dragons in Sweden. Landshut brought him in on a three-month contract – that's all they could afford – hoping he would attract the kind of sponsorship that would pay his salary for the rest of the year. Which is the deal I gave Hadnot in the book and the reason he eventually quit mid-season and started playing for our archrivals, Würzburg. This is what happened to Johnny. Würzburg was also, in fact, the club that Dirk Nowitzki actually played for, so the two of them became teammates in the end, and their rivalry was real.

I liked Johnny and wasted a lot of time arguing with him about stupid shit, as you do when you spend your days on buses and in locker rooms, waiting for games to start or to cool down after them. He was, in his own way, a born-again Christian, who carried a Bible with him on road trips and took notes about details like the number of Hittite soldiers in the battle of Kadesh – that sort of thing. The kind of stats, in other words, a sports fan might want to know about a famous basketball game. He didn't call himself a Christian, though, because he didn't believe in organized religion, although he considered the Bible itself to be the literal and historical truth. So all on his own he wanted to work out what it meant, what it was trying to tell him about how to live. This struck me even at the time as a particularly vivid symbol of the loneliness of an athlete's life. His wife and five kids lived in Texas. A basketball season, including training camp and playoffs, lasts about seven months, which he had spent for the past several years partly on the road but mostly in his team-rented apartment in some small European town, like Landshut or Sundsvall, where he didn't speak the language and where everybody except for a few of his teammates was white.

Here's the kind of stupid argument we used to get into. You can still hear in it the annoying Yale kid that I had been full-time only a few months before. When I asked Johnny what he had learned from his literal interpretation of the Bible, he mentioned the Ten Commandments, *Thou shalt not lie*, all of that stuff, and so, hanging out on retreat in Pezinok, Slovakia, I put to him Kant's test for the Categorical Imperative: what would you do if a crazy axe-murderer knocked on your front door and asked you where your children were? Would you tell him? Yes, Johnny said. Even if he planned to find them and kill them, and you knew that a lie would give him a chance to cool down . . . But Johnny shook his head. Where I come from, he said, that motherfucker would kill my kids no matter what I said.

What happened to Hadnot in the book really happened to Johnny. After three months his contract ran out, and the club decided not to renew it – even though Johnny was clearly the best player on our team. He was also the best player I ever played with, the smartest, too. He dominated people on the court, he got inside their heads; he could do what he wanted with us in practice, day after day. Nobody could stand up to him. But games are a different business, you play against strangers who have no history of giving in to you. Besides, games are over so quickly, the random outcomes of a handful of fleeting moments often make the difference between winning and losing. And we had started to lose. Sponsorship money wasn't coming in, and the club couldn't afford to pay Johnny his monthly rate. So they let him go. There was a fraught team meeting, everybody felt angry, it was like giving up on the season. But Johnny was more than angry. He was being told, in one way or another, you're not worth the money, you're not good enough. And because I spoke German, he sometimes appealed to me to get his point across. I was twenty-two years old, fresh out of college, watching this guy I admired realize (not for the first time, I'm sure) just where he fit in the scale of things: fighting with middle-management in the windowless back office of a third-rate club in a mediocre European league. And losing, because you can't win these arguments. In the book, Hadnot says, 'I'm the best damn player on this team. I'm probably the best damn player in this shitty league. Tell him that, Ben. Tell him that.' But they understood what Johnny was saying anyway, and it didn't make a difference.

In the novel, my father comes to visit me for a week. He stays in my apartment, first on a cot in my room and later in my bed, after I introduce him to Anke and start spending the nights with her. In fact, he never flew to Landshut, but he was often on my mind that year, for a number of reasons. It was my father who taught me to play basketball on the court he built in our backyard in Austin – I inherited an old-fashioned wrinkle or flaw in my jump shot from him, a touch of left thumb on the release, which it took me most of that season in Germany to iron out. But he was on my mind for other reasons, too. One of the founding myths of our childhood (I suppose every family has them) involves the story of why we didn't stay in Palo Alto, California, which is where I was born, because my dad was teaching at Stanford at the time. He loved Palo Alto (my mother was happier in Texas), he loved our house and the intellectual life at Stanford, where he was a popular teacher. But he got blackballed at the tenure committee meeting, which was held when one of his best friends and advocates happened to be out of town, and narrowly fell short of the two thirds majority he needed. So we moved to Texas and I grew up in Austin. But the jerk who lobbied against him was always a bogeyman of my childish imagination, and when Johnny fought his corner part of what I heard in his voice was my father's righteous indignation.

The point of his visit in the novel is to tell me, in one way or another, that you can't let these guys push you around . . . He comes to check out some of our gym sessions and notices in me that quality he spent my childhood watching at one high school game after another. A deference that is a kind of retreat, an opting out. (I used to sit on my hands on the bench, looking down, so the coach wouldn't catch my eye and put me in the game.) When he sees me chasing balls for Karl, so the big kid can work on his jump shot before practice, my dad challenges him to a game of H-O-R-S-E. Karl, of course, is my stand-in for the real-life star Dirk Nowitzki, one of the greatest shooters in NBA history. But my father beats him the way he used to beat me, by psyching him out, and I remember writing this scene on a cool sunny and blustery day at the end of March, on his birthday, and thinking, *Happy birthday, Dad*.

I had other visitors to my small apartment up a hill, on the road out of town, halfway into countryside, but they didn't make it into the novel, even though in life I looked forward to their coming for weeks and their company made a big difference to me. One of the things that bugs me about fiction is that in order to make these visits meaningful you have to exaggerate or dramatise them in some way. Rachel, for example, my old hall-mate from Yale, who had filmed me playing basketball by myself on the court at Payne Whitney, stayed with me one weekend. She was studying or working in Germany, living on her own, apart from her boyfriend, who was also a friend of mine. We were both lonely, so one Friday afternoon she took the train down to Landshut and I met her at the station. She slept on a cot in my bedroom. In a novel it might have made sense to play up the sexual tension between us, but in reality there was very little – great liking but no real attraction, certainly on her part, for me. I think I always struck her as slightly loud. But there was still some awkwardness or shyness (sleeping in the same room, we had to decide when to stop talking after turning the lights off and could listen to each other's breathing), which is, in its way, a kind of intimacy. We were both far from home, spending too much time by ourselves, living in a desert of unfamiliarity, where we couldn't ever express ourselves in a casual off-hand way and be properly understood. The fresh loneliness I had set off in that summer had started to change into something else, and I was slightly ashamed to share my studio apartment with her. Twice a day I came back sweaty from practice; the laundry hamper in the bathroom was overflowing; I wasn't used to talking to people who knew me.

In October, the league took a mid-season break and our coach gave us the weekend off. I used it to visit a friend of mine from England who was living in Brussels. (I've just looked it up online: it's about an eight-hour train-ride each way.) We met up with a girl I knew from Yale who was working as a nanny (I think we went to see *Welcome to the Dollhouse*, which nobody liked), and ended up piling into his small studio apartment together, after it got too late for her to take one of the public transport options home. They shared his bed; I slept on the floor. Nothing happened. Another example of the sexual awkwardness and never-to-be-underestimated chastity of youth. This also did not feature in the novel, but when I got back to Landshut I saw that the flowers I had bought for myself (my birthday was on the 23rd) had wilted, and spent the next few afternoons scribbling another poem:

> The lilies I bought to console me on my birthday
> Two odd twigs tipped by pink white pears
> Did not flower before I went away
> On my week's grace, and left them in a jar . . .

I was starting to persuade myself, in the way unhappiness persuades you, that I had to quit.

The last straw fell on the basketball court. One of my teammates was an overweight, enormously tall and ogreish-looking German PhD student, with hanging arms. Everybody called him Big Country, after a

college star from Oklahoma State whom he dimly resembled. Big Country was exactly the kind of player it
depressed Johnny to play with – a natural non-athlete,
who symbolized just how far he had fallen from the
major leagues. So Johnny made fun of him all the time,
he tried to embarrass him. As it happens, Big Country
was the only one of us who ever stood up to Johnny. In
his peevish way he refused to be intimidated. During
practice one night he got fed up and threw a sharp
lumbering elbow at Johnny and caught me instead, just
under the eye. It was like my face had been unplugged
– I sat down and could not feel my cheek. The club
sent me to a hospital in Munich for X-rays, there was a
question about whether or not they should operate. I
was grateful just to be missing practice and by the time
the doctors cleared me to play again I had decided to
leave. It took months for the feeling to return and by
then I was living with a high school friend in Oxford,
scooping ice cream at George and Davis (a local Ben
and Jerry's rip off) and working on a novel. I had also
started dating the daughter of one of my dad's old col-
leagues – we've been married now for thirteen years.

Anke herself played no real part in my basketball adventure. She never came to Landshut and belonged to
the life I had left behind at Yale rather than the weird
first steps of my adulthood. But I imported her into
the novel as a way of dramatizing the conflict I felt
between staying and leaving. My mother and I fought

a lot towards the end, over the phone – she wanted me to see out the season, she thought it would look bad for me to quit, that I would later regret it. And yet as it happens Anke did have an influence on that decision, and for a moment at least the possibility I raise in the novel, that we might have ended up together, that I could have stayed in Germany playing basketball, seemed briefly real.

After packing up my apartment, and shipping or selling or simply leaving behind what I couldn't carry with me, I took a long train north towards Flensburg, which is where my mother grew up. I wanted to spend a few days in her old house, which is still in the family, and which we used to visit every summer as kids. The garden slopes down to the water – you can almost swim to Denmark. But on the way I stopped for two nights in Hanover, where Anke was working, and slept on her couch. Her partner was out of town for some reason – she was living with friends. (I still remember, one of those weird bits of flotsam that floats to the surface of memory for no particular reason and refuses to sink, her roommate sitting in the kitchen eating crackers and asking me, the unusually tall German-speaking American who was spending the night, what my favorite cheese was. Cheddar, I said, and she laughed: Kinderkäse, she called it. Kiddy cheese, and Anke laughed, too.) While I was there, I even tried out for the local club, a second division team in the northern division – dragging wet hi-tops from my duffel and riding another train across another strange town to another game. I did okay, playing with something like my old joy, and might even have persuaded them to sign me on the cheap, if things had worked out differently with Anke.

On my last night, she had a party to go to and invited me along. I watched her and her housemates get ready, the pleasant build-up among friends of social excitement, everybody dressing up. All strange to me, after six months of deep isolation. Meanwhile I had only two kinds of clothes: the kind you can play basketball in and the kind you can't. I think we took a taxi to the party. And I remember making a decision as I followed Anke and the others out of the car, through a lobby, up a flight of stairs – you could already hear the beat of the music – and into a dark smoky crowded apartment. (For some reason, medical students all seem to smoke, and the women wore T-shirts that said things like *Destruction Is Creative*. It was very German.) I could either spend the night waiting for her to pay me attention or introduce me to people, or I could wander off and practice something I hadn't had a chance to practice since leaving Yale: my ability to talk to strangers at a party. So that's what I did.

Afterwards, on the way home, Anke picked a fight with me. *Why did you ignore me.* I didn't ignore you. *You hardly spoke to me all night.* I didn't want to bother you. You were with your friends, etc. It was the argument we hadn't had in three months at Yale, and which only became possible now that it wasn't really relevant any more. What do you want me to say, I told her. You have a boyfriend, and nothing's going to happen. You just don't want me to go away without telling you how much I like you.

Maybe that's true, she said. What's wrong with that.

We both went to sleep in a bad mood and in the morning had to get up early to catch different trains. (Mine towards Flensburg – I can't remember where she was going.) It was cold out, a northern late autumn morning, and we wrapped ourselves up in thick clothes that made it easier not to talk as we walked to the station. I thought, this is stupid, it shouldn't end like this, but before I could change the tone we had bought our tickets and separated according to platform. I couldn't see her any more, there was a train in the way, the train to Bielefeld, and I remember thinking that if it pulled out I would wave to her or call to her or do what my mother sometimes asked her kids to do, when we were having a fight: *Guck mich doch mal freundlich an*. Look at me like we're friends. But when the train standing between us eased away Anke was gone.

I've lost it now and don't remember any of the lines, but that was the last poem I wrote in Germany, about the train to Bielefeld, which suggests that I was fed up enough with the whole business, those miserable months of my life, to look back on them already with a certain amount of wryness or tender humor. But they also left a deep mark, a deep stain of failure. Over the next few years I finished first one and then two, three and four drafts of a memoir, which I called *Leagues Away* and which has never been published. It drew on these poems and on the letters from our training camp in Slovakia that I sent to my parents at home. (Sample line: 'You don't know squalor until you've sat in the losers' locker room in Pezinok . . .') Maybe because it was too quiet, I don't know. But the truth is, I don't think I've ever done anything so extraordinary again. People paid me to play basketball in the middle of nowhere and just by chance I happened to play against a seventeen-year-old kid who turned out to be one of the all-time greats.

My mother has a speech she gives to graduating students, and I've borrowed part of it for some of my creative writing seminars. She says that you get to a point in your life when you realize that you, also, are a historical source. That historians might want to talk to you about what you have lived through and seen first-hand. (When she was seven years old, growing up in Germany, the Second World War ended.) I tell my students that this is one of the ways they should think about what they need to learn. It's a question they can ask themselves: of what kind of information am I a source?

Almost twenty years after leaving Landshut, my novel about playing professional basketball in

Germany came out – first in England and then Italy and finally, a few years later, in America. As much as possible I tried to recreate the feeling of the original experience, those *22 blues*, but I failed to stick to the facts in the various ways I've outlined above. By importing relationships and characters from other parts of my life, and building up tensions and conflicts that either didn't exist or found their proper expression at other times. One thing I never needed to exaggerate is the effect that half year had on me. For six months I learned what it was like to measure and test yourself every day in a profession that turns out to be very good at determining what you can do and what you can't – in other words, *who you are*, according to the limited terms of the exercise. But objectively, too, without leaving room for doubt. I was a bench player in a mediocre European league. Anke and I were never particularly in love. Learning these lessons the first time around made me miserable for a while, but I'm happy enough to write about them now.

Partou Zia

– The Notebooks of Eurydice –

The artist Partou Zia was born in Tehran in 1958 and emigrated
to England in 1970. The essay printed here is part of a longer
piece, 'The Notebooks of Eurydice', which Zia compiled after
her diagnosis with cancer. However, Zia had finished much of
the writing before this calamity and she shrugged off the knowledge of her peril as far less important than the act of living.

Zia was deeply affected throughout her life by her state
of exile from her beloved Iran: 'the magical reality I had left
behind on that hot June morning, when I walked across the
melting tarmac, up the uncertain steps to the entrance of the
enormous jet plane' – a land always out of reach. Moving to
Cornwall gave Zia the light of the Caspian Sea and walking
on Dartmoor the mountains of her lost Persian landscape. She
described her life in Cornwall thus:

'Blue sea and stillness; I love this light of soft turquoise
restful in its sense of infinity.'

– Richard Cook

It is a pity we have not alchemical texts written by
women, for then we would know something essential
about the visions of women.
– C. G. Jung in conversation with Miguel Serrano

What would you say other than what has already
been said and is yet to be said so many times
again and again?

In dreams, meetings of unlikely souls are taken for granted, and yet we lead such prescribed circles of existence when awake. Living a story at every given moment, my mind is full of conversations, predictions or memories of other stories, the entire edifice jostling for a place in amongst the many other things seen, remembered or overheard. We are mosaics of thought and sensation, contradictions of memories assembled often upon the least significant 'fact' or 'reality', whilst capable of completely forgetting the things that have happened moments before. The golden tales and stories are with us at every blink of an eye, though we are forever seeking them elsewhere, and at some unspecified time in the future. Emptiness itself is the golden gift we are anxious to avoid.

The great cliffside down to the ocean's drop is carpeted with purple heather; wild flowers and large umbrella mushrooms acting as parasols for the numerous shiny black slugs as they gorge on their late summer's bounty. Thick layers of orange-hued sunset drawn wide across the horizon and the calm pearl-blue summer evening sky gently meeting the velvet green opalescent waters of the cove below. Everything arrayed across my eye's vista as if a memory or a recalling of a hazy memory, or perhaps a snippet of a nameless movie; this reality or factual thing can only be a delicious fiction in which I am to play the protagonist. Fragments of moments, barely assembled into a structured whole; why would I need the false coherence of a tale or morality-play to create interest?

It is the dream-fable that I want to write, *not* stories. A story is the fable dreamed into language. Breaking up of form, and structure, in order to put it all back together again. For example I could begin with: *I dream of giving birth to a half-tiger, half-owl creature; I want to call it Tiger Lilly.*

Perhaps all I need do is to find a name that would call the sky by its true self. But in whose language, and with which alphabet or accent should this naming ceremony be undertaken?

Words begin to well up and form themselves into an army of possibilities, as dusty and rarely opened tomes of memory as yet un-worded unshaped, and almost unremembered. Until it has been framed into a particular pattern and taste, memory is an inanimate thing. It cannot exist simply as a series of images, encapsulated through time. It is the Word that makes memory *become*. And that is my task: *to shape memory into a becoming.*

It is the greatest adventure to make concrete the gesture of one's innate realities.

Moments of purity are taken up by the practical. I am beset by pain and exhaustion, and as a cure I eat to fatten myself. To drift into the poetic is in itself work. The only worthwhile 'knowing' is Memory, or else there is only the false knowing of factual components and measurements. True knowing is not merely to serve a

In Accord II, 2007, oil on canvas

purpose or fill a gap in understanding. Living on the brink of the edges of knowing, fear pervades in a curious haze: fear of the great void into which the self, imagination and memory disperse; and the mystery of being within unknowingness.

A buzzard, dapple-earth-coloured, perched on a telephone pole, cannily eyeing the barren country roads crowned by a ribbon of mathematically-arranged wires that stitch earth-horizons with the wide sky. Hours spent in bed reading, my only solace. Outside is alien, and I am too vulnerable to venture forth

– stay and be protected in the Word. Music hurts me, and the creaking silence of the apartment jars. Sleep is the only place where I can forget and become myself. I spend the day asking the most infantile questions, to which no answers are returned. Why do the waves roll and curl each moment anew? Each night the tide comes up and, never ceasing, never asking questions, the earth turns. Where is the great source of Meaning? Who or what gives instructions for things to happen? The stars shine and the wind blows, people die and still others are born. What would happen if the great 'machine' were reversed, and night became day; if the moon emerged at dawn and the sun shone at dusk? Amidst all the Greater Meanings, there are those who construct the secondary scaffolds of government, rules, economics, cruelty, and power – that other mighty thing, of which much is said, usually by those who do not possess it. What is 'infinite intelligence', if not detached from all of this? Does God, whose attribute is this abundant intelligence, have a memory, or an unconscious instinct?

What are the magical beginnings of language; how has the meaning and sound of a word become shaped so as to correspond with the thing pointed at, described, named? We are now so far removed from the heady days of discovery, having lost the connection between the beauty of a tall majestic ash, its silvery leaves dancing in the blue sky, and the desire to shape our mouths into the word TREE, awake to the sensual groping of roots set deep in the earth beneath our feet. Time betrays our understanding and it is so much simpler to just accept the categories and convictions as we have inherited them, without considering things of which we can never be certain.

There is always an illusion that one is the un-named observer or unseen protagonist. Equally so, that one is being watched as much as one is watching; the importance of I to the thou being only balanced by the placement of that I in relation to yet another: thee. The one who is in the role of seeing is there-fore never truly invisible, [the] *I* to *thou* to *thee* are all interrelated; observation is not a solo activity. At any one moment, there are eyes upon eyes, some aware of the other, while others not even recognising the multi-dimensioned blinking performed around them. Being observed on the other hand, is not only when one is visible to the other, but even a single sighting or a name attached to an unknown or unseen person, a position, a title, will suffice to instigate the chain of watchers watched by watchers, etc. How others view me is both a mystery and a nonsensical equation. Why should I care? Opinions are not perceptions of the true eye.

Despite the intrinsic beauty of neatness, it is al-ways the misshapen that draws me in. Another thing, if you must speak in tongues then do so with courage and not with apology, there is no disgrace in knowing they have all been here before, and that now it is your small turn to reveal the overgrown path, to track a new road. Taking the word and making a music that rhymes out of dissonance a language that speaks of many past lives, one that is formed from left to right mingled with yet another that is perceived from right to left. There, somewhere in the middle with both hands working, a sound that configures an image of true authenticity. I speak the ambidextrous line of words marching towards the centre of the page, to a place of meetings and so the pivot of the circuitous begins.

Rain. Moon. Darkness. Shadows. Moon. Bird Flight. Dawn Chorus. Cat brushing past a rosemary bush. Clock striking the Hour to Rise.

The sea blots out Time. The sea clears out Memory. Here the simplest detail comes to relive its existence. December 10th, 1798, Sir William Hamilton's cargo of priceless vases is wrecked and sunk off the Isles of Scilly. Last night I felt my shadow had changed; as I turned to go indoors my shadow surprised me, blotted in synchronistic motion alongside my step as an alien being I could not recognise. Who is this wild-haired woman striding forth in the dark? Tonight, the sea is troubled, and shrill, the dark night waters churn and turn against the soft underbelly of the ocean floor.

In the dark vast middle-night, that sickly feeling of being abandoned and condemned to a life of obstacles makes everything appear pale or faded. Instead I try to calm myself and recall St Anthony's in Gillan, locked inside a milk-churned atmosphere of low tides slipping over mud flats. I am lost in the green fluting of light that moves up and up with trees and foliage all tapering into the vast distance up above my head. The slithering current of the creek keeps me content in its delicious formlessness. Perhaps all that we know will in time be forgotten, and then what? Meantime we hold on to a sense of calm, and I forget how to pray. If Time is a convulsed, unbounded, irregular, non-linear *thing* then surely place or space can hardly exist as a complete, finite, fixed, known, grounded quality considered as being of and within Time. Could it be that this thing we express as space relies for its possibility on the intimate imagination and willful awareness of the body in movement, therefore through this interaction with a material mass, gaining a 'reality', or knowable substance. I am not implying that everything is therefore subject to myth, a story, or a non-'truth', but I am asking: . . . then how? The universe is fast moving away from itself and everything else around it. There is a great shattering taking place, at this precise moment, yet I sit here assuming the static, the untouchable, unchanging aspect of the quiet of things, the earth, and stars. We are all so mistaken about Time, and Space, and Energy. How wonder-full and how awe-full the reality of this fast self-destructive dynamic is. And over and beyond that, we are all intent on further annihilations of each other. Indeed what great wisdom and leaning we have accrued!

Shadows are those who make with Colour a shape resembling nothing. Shadows are those who make with Word a reality that only truth has tasted, turning it again and again in its sad mouth. Shadows are those who make with Breath a chord that no heartbeat can tolerate. Shadows are Silence sung in chorus. Shadows are those that Name defies. Shadows are Travellers whose luggage stays at home awaiting their return, moving slow against the current of Time.

I look up and the veranda flutters clean linen in the midday heat; the house steams with clothes being washed, vegetables cleaned and put to dry, women talking of nothing in particular, and inside the shut-tered rooms all is dark and cool. Rushing, always rushing back and forth and, it seems, never arriving anywhere. The individual is hard to take. No obliga-tion to stifle myself in order to be given so-called 'love': I stand. I stand. I stand. Family, lover, friend and col-leagues force one into the *known*, the *congruous*, and the *familiar*. They help to mould and mark the appar-ently personal gestures on our faces, in our person, but they would as happily tear us limb to limb, than let us *Be* ourselves: as an unknown, dangerously ambiguous and uncommitted Self.

I am homesick for that place which holds my past and birth, marking my myths and smells that go beyond memory. Being a foreigner is a painful weight that I have learnt to carry with grace, but now I want to set it down and walk away from it. I am not merely a guest, I am a stranger, an unknown, who has outstayed her welcome by taking the guise of her host country, though still never quite so disguised outwardly as to forget the language of her heart's need. The stark reality is that I am neither of the here nor of the place I journeyed from in childhood; it has come about so that now I belong to no people or place.

As

    You

        Go

            Don't

                Forget

                    To

                        Breathe.

—

Browsing through the richly fascinating 'Notes' to Rilke's *Elegies and Sonnets*, I come upon a long letter to Lotte Hepher (November 1915) – speaking of death, the weft of which is woven with the same thread of truth as that of life: is this a good example of the synchronistic or just 'life'? And everywhere around us, death is at home, and it watches us out of the cracks in Things.

I remember the wide-blue infinite depth of life, high above the mountainous paths, always surging, sheer green shimmering between the shadows and space, or the sun-soaked nights of summer and the scent of midnight heat mingling in the evening breeze. Rocks edged together, held tenuously by coloured rags, nets and old canvas embellishing greys of granite, dark, dank black monoliths spangled bright. Here and there, bright broken pieces, the remnants of a boat, once a happy vessel now long drowned by sea's flow. Along the free stretch of water, where land merges into sky, clouds lose their identity: white cuffs over the dark wood of masts, peeping out of blue faded denim.

Then surely it is fine to believe that each leaf that falls is mourned by the earth; each full moon that wanes to darkness is mourned by the sky? And I know that the heart of God remembers every blade of grass flattened, every sparrow that succumbs to death in the wintry ice. Nothing goes without notice, though apparent ease deceives the casual eye. Disarmed by the truth of this gentle flow, I relinquish my long vigil and welcome you at my door. No sound audible only warm sweet breath of lungs overwhelmed, and happy heart of my lover's sway, when in stages we swoon in silent unworded love, quiet and each alone; love, my predella of strength and profound relief of heart's stature, towering above a headland of respect, fulfilling affection's dark current of ever-surprising turns. Your smile is a dark Purdah of sorrows, your body smooth and lithe as a lynx, lying still in my arms tamed and powerful. My heart leaps, fearing your absence. Earth-laden heights in the night air mist, curve into unknown distances.

Night time muse of silence, white-halo owl, disturbed from its dark vigil, comes to speak of her preoccupations whilst the rain falls dark and sleek amidst this mountainous wild space.

Walking in companionship though amidst the bliss of word-less-ness, all around us dark woods glisten, and the earth is leavened moist, making a Kaleidoscope of colours. We sit inside the tree with a bottle opened by the wine merchant, heavy cadmium coating our tongues. I am mesmerised by his sandalwood eyes, nestled in the womb of ringed years I grow from girl to woman, transformed. Sparrows, squirrels, shrinking slugs, all gather to witness this marriage of natural circumstance. Time is lost, and I to time the chosen maiden of sacrifice. Sweeping soft smear of sky. Dusk settles gradual orange amidst mellowed greys. Light reflects off the deep-textured tide. Sands resting, dank from the afternoon's watery slumber.

A hasty goodbye, I leave with the fervour of an early return, anticipating your welcoming eyes, honeyed beacons to light my way.

Wind rages. Sea froths, clawing back each wave in a misty splutter of green-greyness. My challenge lies clear ahead. The sun shines on the crisp blue sea. The sky blinks ink-scraped, mauve-bruised and fluorescent over a mass of sea curling white-bright. Waves arched as a liquid arcade coming in again and again over pebbles dry and wet. Like the blustery windswept waves, I cling to the shore wanting dry land to rest upon, and yet the current pulls and grapples me back out to sea. A great chorus of protest as each time a breaker is dragged back across the rocks and pebbles. Back to the wet dark tumult, out there, despite all determination this time to stay. Perhaps each little rock on the seashore is someone lost at sea, or each bird is a bereaved one searching for the lost beloved. How can anything animate or otherwise in nature be a disconnected, isolated atom of essence? Everything shakes violently. Unsettled emotions stir the earth.

How can I take this tiny portion of human existence seriously, when asked to stand and be examined by those who exist at such a distance from the heat of my gaze? Damn this impotent cycle of currency that

Flowering Rod, 2006, oil on canvas

demands my soul in percentages! Go prance about and show off your accolades! Boxes of books; two trunks; thirteen file-boxes; a wooden book case; plants; a statue; several bags, mostly plastic; I am a tourist too.

Outside: the chill cold smell of the sea, enraptured by sturdy cadmium-stained harbour walls, welcomes my surprised heart. In my mind I walk the concrete laden path. Jubilee Pool hangs its head and the old War Memorial, built in the name of death, chastises me. This time I know the meaning behind the signs. We build circles, our very own spheres of lives, protected by the belt of our circles, which we bind around ourselves. Language, anecdotes, mannerisms, habits – we build our circles against the countless faces we pass each day, holding on to the unique belief of ourselves being exceptional creatures inhabiting a unique world. Cutting and shaping our very own exclusive circles from amongst the many thousands that spread outside our given sets of boundaries, swaying in the breeze. A field of the many fades in significance as we cushion snug within our circle, our life, and our dreams.

Remembering rooms perpetuated by sentences; syllables heard in passing. Or the scent of one familiar, whose face you cannot recall. A suitcase, dumbfounded without its cargo of travel, now only an empty carrier of a past everyone wants to discharge, set carelessly in an empty room. The old green curtains flagging the suburban windows, and the unremarkable door with its high-set handle, always stiff to turn. There, in the dim glimmer of an empty room, now vacant of all our pasts, the space groans. The green curtains I remember clearly in my mind. And the carpet, what colour was that? That too was green. Only the suitcase remains colourless, shapeless, and indistinct. Open it and find inside three folios of photographs – a record of lives long dead. Every smiling face has a name. Here is the case that bridged *that* world to *this*.

With the sun combing my lashes, I lounge sleepily against the rocks, on the curl of Gwenver's headland perched overlooking White Sands bay. Surfers like cormorants move up and down the slight silken waves, anticipating the great lift on the lip of turquoise water, turning in towards the beach from out beyond the headland. At a distance almost reachable with one eye shut, sits the Wolf lighthouse, and a hazy silhouette of intrigue on the very nib of this grey horizon salutes the outer plots of the Scillies. Granite headland as our headrest, cream-coloured and speckled with green-grey veins; the monumental rise of timeless rock soaring into the hot sky. Scattered among sculpted boulders out on the beach now deserted in the low tide, are objects landed and marooned, each awkwardly isolated and out of place: large rusted orange tinned vats and opalescent skeins of rope or could it be netting from a boat? Overhead the whirring sound of a helicopter persists, but nothing can drown out the authority of long-ribbon waves crashing inland, possessing boulder and sand. So strong and weighty that despite all appearances this delicate-hued mass of water shifts and rearranges sand and stone within minutes, and that with no great degree of intent. I suddenly see the whole of nature is based on the principle of *Love*: Earth embraces Vegetation and Trees. Water cribbed in the loving arms of Earth. Vegetation as the seat of Birds' poesy, the platform of dance for Butterfly and Insect; Sky and Cloud canopies of protection over Earth and all that it harbours. We on the other hand are rapists and pillagers, appropriating without permission or even decent understanding of this great chain of love.

And in Between
THE unSpoken   and   THE unSpeakable
Rest the Untouched Moments of Unknown Thoughts

Morning cracks a ripe apricot, as colour and light struggle through the grey Sky. The heavens chant morning's choir, saluting Time to awaken and unfurl from the Moon's seductive darkness. The world still recumbent, I settle my heart in the early rain, walking in step with the sun's slow prosody reaching out from a heavily overcast sky. Yes, so we are like the oroborous snake; our task is to reach across our own circumference and bite the tail of our own destiny, meeting the Beyond of ourselves there, hinging the unknown to the conscious self, whilst allowing the empty circular space in our middle to palpitate with Meaning.

Patterns foliate and duplicate themselves from the singular into the many and back again. Each day, waking from the voluptuous land of dreams, we are presented with a universe of possibilities. At this very moment, others are waking to the lactose-sweet cocoon of a newborn child in their arm, or being given news of a death that will change their lives forever. There are those who are still reeling from the night before as the light of day outlines the disasters they have entered upon. Others may be waking up to the fullness of their apparently normal existence as the nightmare it is and making one final resolve to change or readdress the truth of their own meaning. For the most part I expect there is a portion of 'normality' stirring lazily and contentedly in its creased bed linen. Children are seen off to school, young women hopping onto the bus to work, someone washing up to the sound of a favourite radio programme. Newspapers are sold with a smile and a greeting. All this goes on and there are rooms where the curtains will not be opened today, and there are those who will scowl at the pavement as they tread their isolated path, determined to keep their starved souls in the deprived element of spiritual poverty.

We take an impulsive trip to Belston. Blue delicate sky and warm sweet air as we venture along the moors. By 'Jacob's Wall' at the lap of the Taw we rest for lunch. Sunny midday shadows dress everything with the enthusiasm of spring's advent. This place somehow helps to console the great lack that spans between my life and my land of birth; the great nomad-trodden mountain ranges that stitch Isphahan and the miles of magical road to Shiraz. I cannot describe the similarities, only that I am sure that the moors are formed by the same sleight of hand though obviously much colder and far less temperate. These hills and Tors are like the various embodied parts of a great ochre-gold being. A body stretched out in heavenly repose beneath a noble, vast sky. We walk up onto the higher peaks, barely minding the chilled breeze whipping our faces. Land black-burred by fast-footed water, some past blaze and water's wintry fury have gouged an ashen furrow, in place of a pathway. We tread the charcoal curve of ground, at either side greeted by dun-coloured straw that gleams. We look forward to the bloom of the ledged pathway transfigured from passive into active heather ballooned in flowery tufts, each one rough textured and thorn-scented.

New beginnings arrive imperceptibly, almost without notice. It is true then that the river has eyes and each glance of a glimmer rippling its waters affords a glimpse of my mind. I retreat to the 'Towers of Silence' where the clay portraits stare back in elegant repose. Death brings forgetfulness and the dead fade into Time. No amount of reasoning can wipe away this mist of melancholy from the mind's eye, and I feel deeply let down by the elusive thing called life. Every gesture of now-ness is a gift of a lifetime of patience given to you for an eternity of a moment's regard. Time is long, Time is short, whatever height or breadth, Time is a baffling vacuum outside of Self.

After weeks of drowning into the mire of ordinariness, and chores, I am released, fished out by the line of poetry. Each turn brightens my lamp, as it hangs suspended amidst the terrible darkness and wilderness of not knowing, lighting my way gently as I journey 'from the alone to the alone'. Every step pre-mapped on the watery ridges of the unexpected topography with the pencil of hope and desire. In this way I am taken from station to station, without effort, to be led towards my destination.

We walk to the flint field. Overhead the ambitious whirr of the Scillies helicopter to disturb the hum. Blue Speedwells, white Stitchwort, and gauze of blazing gold. Pink Campions compete with the heartbreaking pink of apple blossoms, garlanding the May sky, and butterflies swoon the air, drunk on the nectar-diffused hedgerows. Three swallows cream-breasted, bills open seducing the insects to fly alongside or near their belly; the gods take care of their divine offspring. We drink tea sitting on a field tucked in the corner at each edge by woods and the white glow of blackthorn blossoms. There as the land slopes down, an emerald handkerchief swaying against the breeze, a fulsome, proud hawthorn tree, seeded so long ago, that I imagine the field and woods that surround it must have happened by way of paying homage to this dowager of splendour. Just out to sea, only a few miles from the shore, water glimmers new answers to questions not yet formulated. In advance of Time I set the alarm button – to waken my self, my life, my voice, and my death. Each representative of a *holy[i]day*, an event for becoming. Gathering momentum as a wave that comes gliding slow, rising up to beat a liquid gesture of tympanum against the pebbles, resounding the harp-leaved seaweed into the soft powdered sand. There it curls into the air – clear water – free – Avanti! Spattering spluttering splintering speaking: I begin to roll, rise and become *wave*: something open, and specific, not held to any known form, and always ahead of myself.

Early hours of the morning, my neck stiff, and my eyes red for want of sleep. Last night I finished reading *Moby-Dick*: an over-lengthy text, infuriatingly detailed, beautiful, memorable and in so many ways the most significant thing I've read to date. Don't ask me why or how, as only when blessed with old age will I be able to say exactly what I mean by that. After months of waiting, the Time of Times is here for me to begin my journey towards a future already spelled out by everything but Time itself. How can we arrive before having even set off? And look! The world doesn't end, no, in fact there is every sign that it goes on no matter how much one worries. Blackbirds: ecstatic, robust in their protest. Sing, my yellow-beaked one, sing!

Up above the small sea-town, he picks me a posy

of deep yellow flowers, 'Corn Marigold' – 'introduced in Neolithic times,' and, my face lost in their powdery ochre sweet reminiscent of marzipan, I wonder if they smell as sweet as then. Two little girls on the stone steps leading to the churchyard paint their toenails electric blue, and giggle unceremoniously at every passer-by. The substance we call Life is thick and often a strange thing in our hands. I push and knead it, press and pull it, and yet it seems only the slightest effect emerges from all my efforts and struggles. My being is wrought and compressed under the strain of getting this thing called Life to conform to some shape or notion. So far I've managed to separate and define only the most miniscule portions that stand as independent parts of an unruly, difficult whole. These I call family, affection, morality, ethics or conduct, and home. Whilst the parts I have the greatest struggle with are pride, and money.

Grey mists veil our newly entered bliss, with a pearly delight. Our whole sense of self and each other is transformed, having made our sacred vows of holy matrimony. I am surprised at myself; we are both bound in a charmed bond held within this new-found closeness; pride of love and goodness warming our hearts. What bliss to experience being happy in the silence of this wilderness – as a healing and nurturing balm to our years of work and struggle. Here we are and how good it feels too. Despite a world of fears housed in my mind, I am sure that 'all manner of things shall be well'. Each night I go to bed unwell, and wake up much more hopeful of my health. Still I feel no tangible improvements as such: though I believe only the best will be. It is nearly the end of May yet I sense a new year is only just beginning, this an advent of self and psyche more than time and calendar. The lunar and solar changes are more thrilling when observed from within than merely annotated as passing of the days, time years and so on. I just hope to god that my health improves and I go on to live a long and creative life. At this present stance I am not sure of the future. By six in the evening rain stops, sky clears and a soft May light settles on all things: I am certain Hope is near. A beautifully calm sunny day, and we walk to a new spot along gloriously colourful lanes with hedgerows abundant and smiling. A place that is more like unveiling one's way through a soft and luscious fold in a dream. Peaceful time spent on our flint field – which is grassed or sown with some pretty mauve flowering growth, and therefore prevents us to really look into the ground for flints. We eat lunch out in the open. How I love the wilderness of Cornwall, the untouched quality of these lanes, may it be so always. In the calm of the spring I realise that I have risen from the ashes of self-doubt, fear and despondency into an almost *nothing*. After the weeping and the cold shivers, I regain my confidence and taking the shroud I shake and tear it into strips, and throw the whole ugly inheritance onto the pyre of old wounds. The gloaming of these

Self-portrait in Tresco, 2006, oil on canvas

flames will now be visible as a warning from miles around. Today I awake and softly catch my shadow in the morning-shadowed windows. 'You've come back a different shape' – true, I have indeed. Suddenly my voice returns, and with it a strength that is better rooted in my centre. Out in the garden early, and everything scents ANEW.

What is a lifetime if not mostly waiting? I spend hours and hours of my existence in a kind of suspension, part ailing with physical exhaustion, or financial worries, and part attending to bland though necessary chores. Then after days of being locked out of myself, negated to even the sense of what it is to be permitted a 'look in', I snap open. There within the hub of a few moments perhaps a few hours, something changes and the locks snap open. I enter the arena of touch and silence though managing to remain in some kind of aimless self-control. Contradiction rules in this place. But it is the place also where things really begin to find a voice and colour of their own. I enter disbelieving half thinking that I shall be told to leave and wait for the next time, and I already see how I will be forced to leave without the promised thing. Each time I fear if there will ever be a next time. I stay very still; showing no intentions on my own part; no will power betrayed. Let it all become as it must with designs of its own, well beyond anything I could plan and devise. I can wait. This last waiting is the most fraught. Then a wave of light and air softly passes over my face. My hands begin to do what they need and I simply follow. Nothing is needed here. I leave my ambition, my ego and my schedules outside of this place. I am greedy, and yearn to exist inside the *wall* of this sanctuary unannounced. The time permitted me is always limited, and I must take what I am given. Afterwards everything outside of the here seems as though guided by a ventriloquist, and I feel remote to myself, yet lacking a mistress, to make my various aspects function as a whole. It is like being perched above the highest mountain and listening to the gods whisper in private discourse. The gods laugh at my childlike greed as I ask to be held forever in that sacred height, and I sense my self falling and falling, a tired, wordless sensation collapsing down deep into myself.

Tired out.

Sunday, quite late in the day driving up towards Porthgwarra we come to a halt, as synchronistic audience to a remembrance ceremony, with four neat rows of local village folk standing to attention in the middle of the tarmac road, awaiting the strike of the eleventh hour. The vicar, the local councillor, local parishioners, and a few of the residents standing in their front gardens each neatly attired, with poppies in their lapels observing a universal decree of silence. The grey tarmac winding through the village, past the undistinguished village hall seemed to have emerged out of a vacuum of time, and despite the crude presence of cars stopped in a line of disarray, this quiet country road transported us all into an imaginary bond of union and mutual respect. Flags flying high fluttering gracefully in the warm sunshine made of this public solemnity a modest festival. We too stood out in the soft autumn air, obediently close to our car. The three-minute silence over, a determined little speech broke the spell: *'we give our today that you may have your tomorrow.'* Irreverently I am reminded of Captain Ahab's monologue as he observes the decapitated head of a large sperm whale suspended to the side of the 'Pegnod' – *'Speak you venerable head . . . and not one syllable is thine'* – evoking a beautiful moment of revelation out of Ahab's personal bitter rivalry with the poor dead creature. How insignificant all of life's incessant activities, assumed powers and sought after knowledge or fleeting prestige once death has *spoken*!

—

The Art of Being:

Discipline. Concentration. Patience.
Breathing the I-ness of myself.
Sincerity.
Being aware of the now . . .

Silly thoughts of death in the idle of the night, and then a crystal moment of understanding, and I stumble upon something I had looked for all my life. Intrinsic revelations often take place in the most dull and uneventful ways. No name, No description, just a connection of self to place to time. After this, I somehow feel freed and more relaxed, with neither anxiety nor fear of the future. It seems that all time has turned into a solid state, things have stopped and Time is held as a statue at the centre of me. The 'big' things are all that matters, and around them the 'little' things somehow all begin to fall into place.

Memory: Untraceable
Time: Unforeseen
Remembrances: Unprepared

The blue out there comes to me as a vast abstract col-
our-messenger: and so begins a day of ornithomancy;
a bird flies against the window, though the thud leaves
no trace of its momentary presence. Later three little
girls crouch inquisitively over a dead bird by the seashore. I hear the warning call of a small bird behind
me, yet, turning round I can see nothing but a brick
wall, mouldy and badly in need of repair. I feel delicate
and weepy. My heart is softening to thin gauze, easily
bruised by the slightest criticism. Reading poetry I realise – not without irony – the invisible license TO BE
is now mine. Sitting in the light of dawn I feel that I
have no way to say what I want to say. But in time I will
begin to find a source of warmth that is slowly moving
towards me, and language as it is *not* spoken begins to
settle on my lips.

Hovering at the centre but often taking residence
at the periphery. I hover and linger unsure and at the
edge of things. Will I fall off and slip in a circular
dive into the abyss never again to be privileged with
the possibility of emerging up onto the rim of things?
Would it matter either way? How I used to mock the
notion of age taking one's vitality and now I know the
taste of that loss. The moment the desire for escape
enters my mind I suddenly come to myself and stop

quite still, concentrating my gaze at the most mundane crack or the grooves of mysterious tracts on my skin. I must not run away. I must simply remain and wait for the next day, patiently learning to count the bricks along an unremarkable façade, or take special note of the passers by in yet another street of no special features. Stay and be content because evening will soon be here and things will be easier or so the dark stars promise. In case you have forgotten let me remind you what the Talmud says:

The World Is As We Are Not, But Rather As It Is.

Dusty road, and eerily empty corridors swirl around me, and I thought I saw a baby on a counter for sale. So concerned with the world I forget the world. It is not the world of water smells and daisies shining in the rain. Let it all go is what I hear myself say – just be and write and paint and be. God's affection can work in dire ways: by hurting and oppressing by killing by giving you a disease, by keeping you from your goals, by so many ways that are too innumerable to list. Degradation, hurt, or humiliation are not disciplined aspects of spiritual practice, accepting them is only a kind of passive resignation to 'the way of the world'.

Boats boom their farewell call sliding out of the harbour's gap leaving for skies that shine bright and hot. I welcome the ordinary in hope of the ecstasies, the momentary gems that can so easily be missed. Living a romance is not an option. Reality has a sharp taste that is addictive. Timing and an ability to keep the core of your intention in front of you is the only way to survive. Time for the poetic must be snatched and held onto with care. Everything conspires to smother one with mediocrity. Be Ware!!! In church and something spoke to me of my ways and discreetly nudged me on the shoulder to mind my moments, and appreciate my life's every breath. I wake up to see the light kissing the rim of the plastic kettle, the scent of rain from the night before, and the blessed silence of my own life, my studio's colour-splattered grey walls, and so much more that rose up and greeted me with a new urgency: every glance, every breath, every gesticulation, and every fruit bitten into could be the last. I begin to learn to be awake, tingling with presence.

It is Light that varies our seeing senses, our emotions. When bright and clear, space opens out. When dulled and deprived, all seems to shrink inwards; suspicious and closed up. I have faith in the birds, the flies and moths. I have faith in the plants, the dishes, and even the forks and knives, to protect me at times of distress. I have faith. The trees are swaying violently in the Wind, and their sound is a melancholic moan; almost like the waves of a lovesick Sea. Last night I dreamt of someone saying to me: 'Don't purse your lips together so tight.' Gradually I learn to become convinced of my lack of conviction. What is 'right' decides itself. After all did the process of evolution occur after a decision that it should? The tide of Life is stronger than the ebb of one's mind. I feel certain now that uncertainty is the core of all progress and greatness of touch. Of that one thing I am certain, and the rest is the humility to forget one's name. The other discovery of any authenticity is that I am sure the certainty of the hours spent in sleep bears no truth on the uncertainty of dreams. The pity of it is that I so often cannot decipher the code given, except when looked at through the uncertain or the unknown; a jigsaw of unlimited pieces with which I am content to live in waking life.

Continue to believe that it is possible to speak as one dreams: that the analytical can also be imaginative and not always so consciously committed to the 'known' aspects of life. It *is* possible to hedge the given or the apparently solid with real thinking. In the meantime, how to learn to trust that despite dire state of finance there will be enough to see one through life? TRUST, TRUST, TRUST. The cool brisk totality of all that lives around my presence begins to pervade my every cell, calling for compassion. I yield and in an instant, as in a vision, I sense the absolute union of self to other. In a sudden realization I decide, I become, I am completely opened out to the purity of body, spirit and hence the love of *That* which is also *This*. I no longer need my mannerisms or attitudes, and as a garment long grown too tight for my spirit I strip down to myself. Tonight I pack my soul's bag and depart to another place and a different element altogether, no longer belonging to what I was. Instead, Purity, Presence and Poetry – is where I am bound.

Anakana Schofield

– The Difficult Question –

Es ist alles lächerlich, wenn man an den Tod denkt!
– Thomas Bernhard, 1968
(Everything is ridiculous, when one thinks of Death)

Every evening we are poorer by a day.
– Arthur Schopenhauer, *Studies in Pessimism*

PART 1: FUNERAL

It rained the Thursday in 1976 that we buried my
father. I was six. I recall that it rained because
the top of his coffin displayed splodges of water as we
prayed over it. I wanted them to hurry up and lower
him boxed because I worried the rain would soak
through the coffin lid and make him wet and uncomfortable. The rain might rub out his features, erase him
faster, and he would not rest in peace. His soul needed
to leave his body and if he were sodden inside that
box then how could his soul escape? I remember this
water anxiety because the priest dampened him even
further by inflicting the traditional holy water flinging
that happens at Catholic burials. A metal wand was
plunged in and out of a holy pot as the priest doused a
blessing motion over the grave. The wand was placed

into my six-year-old hand and I too was invited to disperse holy water on top of his burial box. I batted it at my feet and let holy water bless my red Clarks sandals instead. This was the amount of control I had: four splashes of holy water. It would become a metaphor for my writing life.

In my, it must be said, mostly pessimistic notions of utopia, funerals do not take place when it rains and memories of them do not include rain. People would die according to the weather forecast. Tears are the rain. There's no need for rain when there is tears. Ask anyone. They'll tell you this. They will nod their head as they speak it. Memories should not and do not include rain. We'll agree on that much.

My father died very suddenly. He had been killed in an accident. The aircraft he was in had come down onto the embankment of a motorway. Many passengers survived, but my father was one of the three who did not. There was no clear reason why he didn't escape based on the seating arrangement in the plane. We have since wondered if he deliberately didn't move (unlikely) or he let someone push ahead of him to help others (more likely) or he had a heart attack en route to impact and was dead in his chair and could not move (the most likely). The Transportation Safety Inquiry, definitely not as rigorous as it would be today, revealed he was found still in his seat with safety belt fastened, so this meant he didn't die saving someone else. He died refusing to save himself. For years and years and

years, I would ask why didn't he move? Maybe he
didn't like us. Maybe he was tired. Maybe he was pray-
ing. Maybe he had another family. Maybe we were not
worth living for. Maybe. Maybe. Maybe.

My mother had returned from working a late shift
in her factory job to learn the news. I don't know who
delivered it because she has never offered that information. She doesn't offer much information on his death.
This immediately provokes even more curiosity. Even
the local media came sniffing around his case, but
grew tired of her unwillingness to reveal even his age
or place of birth and they disappeared to report on the
local fireworks display and a bank burglary instead.
The problem was my father had not told my mother
he was taking that plane or any plane. The first she
knew of this plane trip, he was dead. She said she never
even thought to ask where had the plane come in from
because she was bone exhausted after work and stun-
dered by the idea he could ever be dead, much less that
he was actually dead. He was thirty-eight years old.
She only thirty-two years old. The marriage had been
frowned upon because my father was a Muslim and
she a Catholic. This explains my strange name. One
child would be given a queer name, that was all she'd
allow him. The others would be named for Saints. My
mother tells the story that they had fought because she
wanted to name me Joan for Joan of Arc. 'You were an
ugly, blue looking baby and I didn't think you'd live
if we hadn't put a strong, determined name on you.'

My father prevailed saying he would not have any girl of his named for a devil worshipper. My mother told him to shut up and eat a biscuit. For years they would laugh about this story every Christmas when the tin of Kimberley biscuits arrived from Ireland. The biscuit, ginger with mallow filling, would be waved my direction and my father would jest. You are lucky! If your mother had her way you'd be named Jacob or Cadbury and then he'd tweak my nose. I hated this thing that he did. It hurt. Everything about my father hurt.

After he died, my mother never referred to him as merely *dying* or *having died*. My husband was '*killed*' in a terrible accident was how she described it. Forces outside of her had stolen him from us. He didn't die a death. He was killed. A death was imposed on him. All she would say of this mysterious plane ride was that *what was done was done* and she had no interest in learning what he was or wasn't up to. *I choose to think kindly on it* she'd say *because I have four monuments around me to him. His children.* If she discovered any further grim detail she would lay down and never stand up. *I would be following him into the grave and then you'll have no parent at all.* She was a practical woman, my mother.

Her one concession was to never step onto a plane. *I don't trust them. They are not safe.* Anyone who knew her situation would immediately concur. *They are not, they are not at all.* Once some jester, unfamiliar with the scope of her tragedy, made a Smart Alec comment about the *Titanic* and safety. She withered him with such a look he shut up. I learned the power in a firm lipped, silent stare.

We will carry on as God has intended was her Monday to Friday command.

I, however, chose, by age seven, to amend the official story and told anyone who asked that my father had died in a war, in an aircraft, fighting bad men with bayonets. I made the mistake of telling another girl at Brownies this story and adding the unfortunate detail that it had happened last week. This did not work out well. My mother was very, very angry when a direct phone call came to offer sympathy on this very recent death. A phone call of supposed consolation that was actually a phone call of information, intended only to report on me and highlight I was making things up. Not that I was entombed in what was unmistakeable grief.

The night my father died, my mother did not sleep. I know this because I woke. It was unusual. I never woke at night[1] even though I had trouble falling asleep. In the living room the (outlined) trace of people sat. One was a priest. Sandwiches. Someone had made sandwiches. Someone always makes sandwiches when the news is bad. All talk ceased when I opened that living room door. The fire was on. I saw that, before I saw any person sat there. The fire. My mother sat low to

1. Now as an adult I wake every time it rains. Since we live in a rain-forest I am rarely asleep.

the right of it. Crumpled shape to her spine like she'd been viciously kicked and was guarding her stomach from further attack. Her face was blanched, but she let on nothing as she immediately lifted from that couch and scooped me out of there. Up the stairs she said muttery mammy things about bunnies and ducks and that we were going back to sleep because the bunnies needed me in the morning. Our rabbit, an ugly cobbled brown creature indifferent to human affection, had been killed rather savagely by a rat, so the bunny reference these forty years later still confuses me. But I respect that she invoked me as necessary to something or somebody, the affirmation that I had a function as soon as the sun rose. When it did rise, I was sliced in half. Not only was my life severed by the loss of a whole parent, but also the childhood I possibly might have had was amputated and divided by much more than fifty per cent that night. When two parents become one parent that equation is obvious. But when the main wage earner's pulse is cremated inside an aircraft your economic prospects wholly burn with him.

PART 2: IMAGINATION

None of the above detailed is true, except one central fact. I present it this way to demonstrate one of my queries in this essay. The imagination: Our access to it and increasing devaluation of it.

PART 3: THE TOUGH QUESTION

In fact I did bury my father in 1977 at the age of five and a half.[2] I was entirely absent from the proceedings and all I recall is staring at the grass and people's feet and thinking it all took too long but I enjoyed receiving presents once we were back at the house. Now I recollect the receipt of these presents with heavy sadness, as though the acquisition of a plastic game of peg Solitaire might assuage, even momentarily, being severed in half.

Each year I fail to register my father's anniversary. I am now forty-five years old. That's 39.5 years of forgetting the date. That seems like a terrible thing. Will anyone remember me when I am dead? I very much doubt it based on my own record of remembering.

I have written three books. Two novels and a paste-up art book. That's my actual 'record'. They are

2. Actually I have just recalculated it. I was six and a half but for forty-five years I thought I was five and a half when it happened.

the only entity that has recorded or records me. It's the only way anyone will encounter me once I am dead. Except, of course, they do not record *me*. They solely record my imagination. That's what readers encounter. Only handwritten letters or personal emails absolutely record me. I won't leave any letters for anyone to hear me. There will be no letters. The delete button should take care of the rest. The prose will remain. That's it. Comment c'est.

'I do have one question and it's a tough question,' the radio journalist wrote. It wasn't a tough question. It was an irksome question. 'Do you know a man like Martin John or the women he has victimized?'

Are you in that book was really the question. Or is the man in your recent novel, *Martin John*, is he your father or a relative? No I am not in that book would be my strained reply. I am alert and breathing in the world. I am surrounded by some of what is in that book. Is it less valuable now that you have established my father was not a sexual deviant? Should I make this easy and answer the 'tough' question as one friend suggested by saying why yes, like the character in my novel, I am a dangerous sex offender. If I am a dangerous sex offender is my novel about a sex offender more valuable? Would the implied authenticity or authority actually raise its literary merit? I believe we are currently in an intellectual weather system where it would. The rise of the memoir, the increased emphasis on the personal confessional have led us here, to this time, where not only does the biographic usurp the imagination, but the market demands the writer (disproportionately it seems if she's female) provide it. Fiction has more market value if it's backed up by an additional justification for its existence. The acceptable/ideal justification is: I, the writer, have lived this or some part of it.

I am not inside that book *Martin John*. It is comprised wholly of my imagination. I am here typing things to you, making paragraphs up to demonstrate that I make paragraphs up.

I should have replied to that journalist's question:[3] I am under the ground. In order to make that book I am inside it, in so far as I am under the ground with it, buried by it, ruined by it and my blood has been thinned by it.

Who cares, right?

No one cares mammy.

That's the echo of my son, *nobody cares mammy, nobody cares* he'll chirp. My son has only ever buried a hamster and fish in his life so far. He says he feels no urgency. This puzzles me. Where is his sense of desperation? Where's the despair? This relentless yet propulsive despair that bangs out and inflicts these lines on you. Would he feel more urgency if I were dead? Is that even a reasonable question? Do I feel more

---

3. I take no issue with the journalist who asked it since that's her job, just as mine is to shape discourse around literature and to that end my curiosity extends more to what has given rise to this question & the chronic conflation of fiction & life.

struggle, excessive urgency on account of those early images of wooden box lowered into the ground that had a dead body in it? Has my life since 1977 been defined by the idea there's a coffin being kept warm for me and that each day I am not inside it is merely one day less I will remain outside it. Life as a count-down only to death. I cannot even afford a coffin. My son would have to bury me. Then he'd feel urgency or not. I wouldn't want him to feel that urgency. Here are the contradictions of parenthood. I am typing them to you.

PART 4: CONTRADICTIONS

The contradiction of life is death. The contradiction of writing is time. If I could do formulas there probably is one, but I cannot even manage Roman numerals. If as soon as you are born you're a day closer to dying, we are basically all dying all the time.

When something affects or is bound to affect us all we tend to discuss it.

Yet death covers all of us and is not our daily dis-cussion. Only the thanatophobes keep that pot boil-ing. It's a pot that has a single and unusual internal burner. Self-fuelling.

PART 5: VERIFICATION – A CAVEAT

I feel I must propose an honest indication of verification within the essay for you, the reader, because I
have playfully deployed fiction as our/a starting point
to raise my objection to the devaluation of the imagination over confessional and yet, ironically, this essay is
turning into something of the very thing I deplore: the
confessional.

Just as death is impending in life, an argument is
impending within this piece. Might death strike before
I complete this essay?[4] Whatever it is that's impending
in this essay may likewise not arrive. If death arrives
you can verify it. My typing will stop. My typing will
also stop if the impending argument fails to arrive.
You can critically assail the essay as failing to thrive.
Death is not failing to thrive, it's failing to arrive.

To this end I now wish to verify parts of this essay
to you.

Here we go:

Verification begins and I shall indicate when it ends, if
it ends. We won't know yet.

This sentence was typed at 10.51 p.m. on a Saturday
night, January 30 2016, in Vancouver, BC – a sizeable
city on the West Coast of Canada where a dilapidated
house cost $2.4 million last week and it rains far too

---

4. Strangely my daily dose of death anxiety has decreased as soon as I
started rambunctiously and aggressively typing on the topic.

much. Every Saturday night, I type like this, alone in a small, modest, very messy council flat (lucky me, given the $2.4 million) or down the road at the hospital café.[5] Sometimes I fall asleep typing and sometimes I fall asleep reading. I never fall asleep if I want to fall asleep. If I lie down to 'go to sleep', I will surely not fall asleep and only end up restoring the light or reading in the dark on an electronic device because I anticipate falling asleep sooner than is worth stepping out of bed. Normally I give in and remove myself back to the light switch and caution myself, yet again, that there's never any point in turning the light off as I will only have to leap from the bed in seven minutes to turn it back on again. Saturdays are precious because I can work unreasonable hours.[6]

Unreasonable hours are what writing demands. The hours are long, lonely and unreasonable. Ascetic deprivation. A compulsory Simone Weil-ian rejection of fellow humans, daylight and the lights always remaining on after the entire street has gone dark. My street seems to go to bed around 10 p.m. and probably arises at 6 to skip to hot yoga or walk the dog. Since it's Vancouver these aren't unreasonable assumptions.

5. This addition was actually typed on February 6, 2016 in said hospital cafe, where even the man who sold me the juice I bought said I bet you'd rather not be here and I had to stutter that I'd chosen to be here which made little sense to him I could tell.
6. It's now 8.24 p.m. on Sat Feb 6, 2016. That's not yet what I consider unreasonable, I will let you know by footnote if I am still typing this at 2 a.m. We will verify if I am a truth teller or an exaggerator.

People are outside here. They are active. They are forever on bicycles. I can spend the entire day and night at the weekends and see no one. To further substantiate that I am here typing to you I record that I am concurrently listening to Radio na Gaeltachta[7] which I think I earlier alluded to or will yet allude to in this essay as something I do. Coincidentally it is blasting out of my phone to the right of my ear on a nearby table, but like the light switch I am reluctant to reach over or shift off the sofa to turn it down or off.

The poor night's sleep or poor approach to night sleep, we might attribute to the aforementioned middle of the night thing. My father did die in the middle of the night, I can verify. I wonder now in retrospect how my mother handled the ambulance and the three children who would have been too young to stay alone. Did she go with him by ambulance or who did she call to come and stay with us while she went or was he already dead when the ambulance arrived? I have never actively considered my mother was completely alone dealing with her husband heart-attacking beside her.[8] Was she terrified? Did she know what was happening to him? Did she know how to respond? Should I ask her? By email, by text or phone? I think it would be too difficult by phone. If you haven't talked of some-

7. Traceable here – www.rnag.ie – should you ever wish to join me on a Saturday night in this auditory adventure.
8. I have just verified and verb-ified that he died from a heart attack in that sentence in case you missed it.

thing in nearly forty years could it be a bit abrupt to phone up and demand intrusive details no matter how entitled you might feel to them. But email and text offer emotional distance. Ethically, though, the dilemma returns: do you raise the seams on another's wound for the sake of a good sentence in an essay, do you? I think you do not. That's what I think.

That paragraph though has made the essay more interesting. As soon as I offer some personal truth, some emotive personal truth beyond I had a gerbil and couldn't sing in tune – the essay becomes stronger. Or am I imagining this? Am I also conditioned to Value Added Verification in what I read?

PART 6: THANATOPHOBIA

'Death anxiety (thanatophobia) is defined as an abnormally great fear of death, with feelings of dread or apprehension arising when one thinks about the process of dying or what happens after death.'[9]

What early childhood loss has bestowed on me is an intense, lifelong,[10] acute, thanatophobia. I could

9. Fares Daradkeh, M.Sc., B.S.N., R.N., and Hamdy Fouad Moselhy, M.R.C., M.B.B.Ch., M.Sc., M.D. (2011) 'Death anxiety (Thanatophobia) among drug dependents in an Arabic psychiatric hospital', The American Journal of Drug and Alcohol Abuse, 37:3, 184–8.
10. This essay indicates it's probably not likely to abate anytime soon.

sit on the bus and imagine being dead and not living anymore and it would create something akin to a panicky distress like I was being actively strangled. I recall once experiencing it on a South London bus[11] in my early twenties and recognizing the unusual sound of the Irish language, An Gaeilge, being spoken by two women behind me. This may explain my subsequent and ongoing attachment to that language. I listen to the Irish language radio with the same frequency others pop Ativan, while working to miserable, anxious deadlines for assignments I always regret accepting. Like if I am honest this one. Limited comprehension helps with lessening the distraction factor. If I need to raise my mood I put that language in my ears or I write out the only five characters I can ever remember from the Arabic alphabet.

ا ب ج ح خ ص

ل ت ص ب ح

EARLY BURIAL BY READING

Rogue Male by Geoffrey Household was a novel I studied and the only novel I have any memory of studying for O-level English. It was a profound experience. We

---

11. Failing to verify the bus number here.

had to read it aloud. I was never ever asked to read aloud because I desperately wanted to read aloud. I had to suffer the most awful rendition of this novel aloud, which I duly tackled by reading the entire novel ahead silently. Chapters ahead, I'd read the whole book at my desk, while everyone else was still suffering early chapters aloud. It was a racehorse reading of *Rogue Male*.

Mr Household's novel was a visceral experience. At that time, I read a novel about a man who lived under the ground like a mole. Just because. It didn't matter why he lived under there. I was only captivated by the idea that people could live underground and therefore, obviously, did live underground. Right now. All around me. And because there was an authoritative male voice telling me this, it meant I, too, could go there.

Three years ago, I heard a BBC Radio 4 serialisation of the novel and was puzzled by what I heard. I searched up the novel online and felt a retroactive and horrible kick to the kidney to learn the book was a spy thriller! A classic spy thriller. Episode 5 delivered a sentence describing a man holding sight of another man in a crossfire.

There was no man killing any other man in the novel I read at that school desk. There was no spy on the run. There was just a man who wanted to live underground for a reason that made no impression on me, because I was too impressed by the concept you could live down there. Beneath Clarks sandals. I was impaled on that image. Household could say whatever he wanted after that. I was gone. Underground.

Now though years later, still metaphorically underground, if not writing this essay to you from there, I can see that the reading experience was a possible form of relief to that early introduction to the finality of burial. It was an injection of life. A sous-soil resurrection. That you could go down there and make literature out of the people that lived down there and that, not being the most rationally-oriented child, therefore, there probably were people who could live or were living down there. If I were to re-examine that novel, it might bear no resemblance to the transformative and transporting experience reading it in my youth provided. I'll leave it buried. That reading experience is plain testimony to the intersection of the imagination on and off the page.

BURIAL BY PROCESS

There are people who are at ease with dying and there are people whose entire life becomes defined by being ill at ease with it. Thanatophobia has provided me with more than acute death anxiety, it, also, infiltrates and identically mimics my writing process. It is the entire impulse or basis of my writing practice. I am beset by what could politely be termed an 'anxious urgency' about everything I write or have or haven't written and will write. More accurately it's closer to a form of anxious psychosis (functional, since no one has carted me away and I sit quietly at a table and do not suffer the delusion I am Mary Magdalene or Joan of Arc). I finally recently cracked that death anxiety gave birth to not just *a* creative impulse or act, but my *entire* writing life.

It was cracked during a late night, a Saturday late night, like the one I have just verified, where I faced a deadline to write 1,000 words of fiction for a commission that had a nutty one-week deadline and a very specific theme on Human Rights. I needed the 350 euros because it's hard to find 350 euros and here were 350 euros to be had. I had barely managed two hundred words and the piece was due on Monday. The moment of recognition elbowed me as I sat at the table, dispatching emails to the various unfortunate sets of virtual ears who put up with me, that *I haven't written anything and holy fuck what am I going to do?*

Yet ding-a-ding-dong I'd felt this precise physiological and mental state hitherto. This arresting debilitation. Yes! It was very recent indeed. It was throughout the writing and even into the copy-editing of my second novel, *Martin John*, until, *ben non*,[12] hold on, I experienced the exact same state struggling for ten whole years to write my first novel *Malarky* and

12. Literally *bien non*. Slang, Québec.

the paste-up art book which nobody read in between and now that I start unpacking the socks and vests of my sombre literary existence to date . . . I have experienced this same arrested terror every single 850-word book review I've ever written.[13] And today, this essay continues to provoke the very same experience. This essay is managing to, yet again, bury me.

What is this burial by process? It is the feeling that Death is coming for me. It's coming early. Maybe today. Maybe before I finish this essay. Type, type, type, quickly quickly type, before it stops me typing. Even once I've typed, I am certain I haven't typed and even if I have typed that there's nothing useful in what I have typed. It's empty and interminable like that Oak coffin I will never afford and yet is waiting to swallow me up. Even when it's impossible to dispute I've typed because it is printed, bound and arrives inside a cardboard box with a price marked up on the back, I continue to experience this mimicked death anxiety. No matter what the papers say, no matter what the editor says, no matter that it's on a shelf – I still worry about that novel. When I see it sat on a table I can only think about the problems that might be in it. The flaws it could contain. Even though if I am honest, at this point my head is usually so fried I can barely recall what it does contain. Sometimes I open my books and read a paragraph to uncover whether it's really as

13. The reviews end much faster than the novels, so there's that small relief.

woeful as my mind has imagined it is or was. Then, and I am sure this has to be common to all writers, upon reading the paragraphs I fail to recall ever having written it at all. If that is endured I move to the next layer of *death is coming for me*, this version though becomes *death is here*. Spadefuls of soil are lobbed onto the imagined plywood coffin. This comes in a neater more straightforward form of *I may never write another book and that if I were to complete one more then I will not worry.* Then I will stop or it will stop. Then I will rest from this incessant self stalking. 'The books are your tombstones,' a friend eating pizza last week cheerfully pointed out.

The reassuring aspect is that no one will notice if I never write another book. This is the great balm of literature and the market indifference to the literary form. *No one cares mammy, nobody cares, talk to the hand*, as my boyo likes to incant.[14]

I was describing this to a friend earlier this week whom I've also embroiled into the operatic saga of not managing to write this essay (note there are already 10,210 words in this document that I keep insisting is not getting written). He interrupted me brisk, puzzled and determined to make sense of it. But creativity is the beginning, death is the end, how can you conflate this act of writing with death? Writing is the beginning of the end, my staid response. He laughed. I chop

14. Here technically verification ends.

my arm, up and down, chop, chop, lay it out for him like the hard lumps of resistant sausage it is. No, no, no, it's not that. It's (chop) early childhood loss, (chop) watching man get put into hole in the ground, (chop) (him: who? Me: my father), (extra chop cos interrupted) thanatophobia, (chop) the process is death anxiety, every time I write I am buried, it's reburial, wham, wham, wham.

But you claw your way out?

No. I don't. It's not that active, more that some vague blip in the earth probably caused by fracking in Alaska or a frisky wolf merely affords a pin-sized entry point for air. Small oxygen.

'It reminds me of a story . . .' and he's off.

See, fiction absolves.

BURIAL BY PROCESS: DISPOSAL

These are the dull mechanics. The mechanics of disposal whether it's onto the page or beneath the soil, there's still a casting off. Polite form involves ritual. Publishing is a ritual, if you are afforded this privilege or trial (perspective depending).

It seems again there is a further replication that happens.

There's the ritual of writing. I suppose it's a utilitarian act of *going to work*. The difference is with writing or any artistic gesture (unless you are contract-ed, which strangely for me in this instance I am) no one is beckoning you. No one says *you must*. It is you *who must*. Because there are so many books, so very many writers (now) it could be assumed that the world would wish you wouldn't. Stop with the books, we're drowning in books. The requirement is to get on with it. For me it's not stagnation. It's certainly not writer's block. It's burial. I dig into a very large hole and then manage to bury myself. I never recall any exit. I just recall confusion. Protracted confusion. I never recall exiting that hole. Except I exit it at some point because otherwise there would be no books and I have pro-duced books. Of course as I am typing to you I am still in the hole.

Inside that hole or these repeated visits to the metaphorical grave, I become very lost. This isn't just an indulgent handy metaphor. I never know physically where my novel is. I lose chunks of it. I chronically make new documents and then forget their names. I print them and lose them all over my apartment. I think I may have written 1200 pages for one of my nov-els. There are boxes of papers, manuscripts, notebooks that attest to it. The reason I know this disposal/burial process takes place is because after the books are pub-lished I can't find certain lines in them. Between the two novels I had a brief concern I had used the word lemon-rind in both. I searched for the instance of it. I had not. I had probably buried the repetition in one of the endless lost documents in one of the endless old computers that ultimately go the recycling and take all the unknown whatever it was with them to be re-formatted and redeployed. Scrub it out, I say. Scrub it out because I only have to go back into this hole all over again.

PART 7: DISTORTION. REAL.

We are all dying basically from the moment we are born. My theory has long been that we should be discussing dying every subsequent minute since so that by the time our hour is up we are utterly exhausted thinking about it and a certain peace overtakes us. Here I verify that in the typing of 'a certain peace' (on February 16 2016) a heavy pressure is felt in my chest like someone is pushing a wooden board against it. Imaginatively it could be oak. It could also be a book shelf, a single plank, but realistically I have to stop typing because it's uncomfortable and I do not like the distress that typing out my one-line-theory provokes and (my pulse is presently 81) must pause for inhale or more verifiably to indulge in some kettle boiling until this passes sufficient to recommence typing.

Someone once pointed out to me that I will not know about dying/death once I am dead. That was quite a revelation, as it had never occurred to me. It brought forty-three seconds of calm, before the holy terrors re-arose and I returned to my default setting, which is 'all will be gone' and there will be no more and it will end. Over. Fin.[15] Rationally that doesn't seem such a terrible thing, since there's plenty to be said for being gone and no longer pondering the more depraved aspects of mankind but even as I type this, my heart rate increases, an uncomfortable clench occurs in my throat and stomach and my eyes squint. It induces a physical tic, which generally takes the form of a head shaking or (left-side inclined) body twitch, a means of the body trying to dispose of this thought.

Death is always chasing the thanatophobe. It's chasing all of us. It's chasing me extra though. It's chasing me for all of you who are not aware you're being chased. I have committed to being extra chased because my appetite for redundant anxiety is accommodating. For most well-adjusted to dying types (ie. not thinking about it or running from it) it's more like a ponderous jog on a seventy-year marathon, whereas for the thanatophobes, or TPs as I will call us, it's like the hundred metres sprint all day long with a fox yapping at your Achilles. A thanatophobe sits in a plane and visualizes, not just falling out of the sky, but burning flesh, bodily disintegration and who will melt first.

15. Enfin even?

We sit on trains. We see them crash as they are gently budging from nondescript stations. That's the point. We see the possibility of death or specifically our own death every corner we turn. Especially when it's quiet or dark. When it is quiet we are particularly afraid. At night it is quiet. At night death can come for us. The thanatophobe doesn't like the night. She doesn't like it one little bit.

It might be concluded the TP has an over active imagination or a reactive imagination or is she facing full frontal what the majority deny? Will their struggle come later or will they be absolved of it entirely because they will not know about death, once they are dead. Grief is for those left behind. Grief is back of the queue. Death anxiety is the chronic queue jumper no one wants to challenge or tackle. Whatever she, the TP, has, it serves the act of writing well. When you do not struggle to imagine the worst, you can posit the very worst. Perhaps you will go where others won't. I do not know. I only know one TP.

PART 8: ACCUMULATION

Grief accumulates and the novel accumulates.

Death doesn't accumulate, unless it's protracted. At the moment of death, however you arrive there, the final breath is the final breath and it just pops you off when it's decided by whatever collection of circumstances that *the* moment is now. That single moment of your very last breath is fast (as long as one breath) and this has an inbuilt equality. Everyone takes a last breath. You are alive. Your pulse stops. You are no longer alive. You are dead. It's the biological full stop. (Pulse 78. Chest pressure hurting). I suppose you could be aware or unaware of that impending last breath in advance, but only those around you actively staring at you can be conscious of it in the *absolute* moment that it happens. Confirmed absolutely just after it's happened. She's gone.

My point is death is coming for everybody. No one is exempt. It is wholesomely inclusive. You can ignore it but it will not ignore you.

Nobody is born without a witness. It's not possible to be born without a witness because you are exiting the witness's body. Even if that woman has died, and you survive, your birth will be witnessed by the person who retrieves you. Imagine in contrast how many people die with nobody bearing witness. And worse still, have no one to bury them.

I find this idea of dying alone, unwitnessed, the most incomprehensible idea. Perhaps akin to never having a single reader.

It's an irrational expectation that death could be otherwise, but fiction writers do not trade in the rational. I can conceptualize a whole economy that could be created to avert people dying alone. People would be paid to be with you, but I fail to imagine how it could be implemented for those who die without warning. Those who die in the middle of the night or those who live alone and there's no one there to be woken up by their passing. It would require a professional observation service of all humans by another human and we'd run out of humans for the task. We could narrow it down to the most likely candidates to die based on illness or genes or not looking the best for staying alive.

I try to imagine the 24-hour shadowing of individuals so that no person would be alone at the point of death and what man/woman-force this would require and grow dizzy. But is it what people want? Do people even wish to have company or their deaths witnessed or do they prefer to be left in peace to get on with it?

Henry James' father felt this way about James's sister Alice. He wrote to her giving her permission to end her life. (She didn't).

'I told her that so far as I was concerned she had my full permission to end her life when-ever she pleased; only I hoped that if ever she felt like doing that sort of justice to her circumstances, she would do it in a perfectly gentle way in order not to distress her friends.'[16]

Since I fear death I automatically assume others do

16. Henry James Sr. In letter to his youngest son, Robertson James (September 14 [1878?]). Introduction, *The Death and Letters of Alice James: Selected Correspondence*, edited by Ruth Bernard Yeazell.

and perhaps this is very much not the case. Perhaps I imagine there's a terror to dying alone that those who do die alone cannot consciously experience. We won't know because we can't know because there are many variables and it's not verifiable. Strange that. Strange that our experience of our very final moment is not verifiable by us. You can spend your whole life analysing and thinking and recovering from your birth. Your death is only for those left behind to analyse. All you get to do is die it.

Intuitively if our final moment will forever remain – to the person who lives it or dies it – a figment of our imagination, then why would our imaginary moments warrant verification? The imagination is devalued when we seek justification for content in fiction. She is redundant, under-employed, within this framework since it's only the imagination that can work up or ponder or create our final moment. We don't demand, nor can we, that someone has lived their final moment before they can imaginatively convey their fears of it to a sympathetic listener. We don't deny them this opportunity by suggesting *nonsense you're only speculating and you haven't lived it yet. Come back to me when you have lived it because only then will it have indisputable value.*

In contrast our present day, self-submission and verifying of every minute of our existence via social media is interesting for the accurate banality it records. It's reassuringly banal. Why we now aspire for that *necessarily* banal testimony to additionally validate our fiction is as mysterious as indulging in a paralysing death complex as a writing process.

More broadly: why would readers seek to verify existence against an apparently created set of fictions? I can understand the manipulation into text of life-based observations as *hidden* source material, but without the tools of literature – language, rhythm, form, syntax, character and ideas – this source material would be lifeless on the page. As lifeless as the endless inquiry to the novelist as to whether this *actually* happened. It suggests to create fiction (that) the writer merely grazes upon herself. Often the answer is depressingly, yes. But even if it is yes, why supply it? Why erase those carefully fought for terms through which we can contemplate serious fiction over the reduction of text to merely you the writer and your circumstances. Language is bigger than you. It's stronger than finding yourself in your own book.

– Notes on Contributors –

JOANNA KAVENNA is the author of several works of fiction and non-fiction including *The Ice Museum*, *Inglorious*, *The Birth of Love* and *A Field Guide to Reality*. Her short stories and essays have appeared in the *New Yorker*, the *LRB*, the *New Scientist*, the *Guardian* and the *New York Times*, among other publications. In 2008 she won the Orange Prize for New Writing, and in 2013 she was named as one of *Granta*'s Best of Young British Novelists.

GABRIEL JOSIPOVICI was born in Nice of Russo-Italian, Romano-Levantine parents, both Jews, in 1940. He lived in Egypt from 1945 to 1956, when he came to Britain. He read English at Oxford and taught at the University of Sussex from 1963 to 1998. He is the author of eighteen novels, four collections of stories, numerous radio and stage plays, and several critical books, including a memoir of his mother, the poet and translator, Sacha Rabinovitch. In 2016 Yale are publishing a study of *Hamlet, Hamlet, Fold on Fold*, and Carcanet a collection of essays, *The Teller and the Tale*.

BENJAMIN MARKOVITS grew up in Texas, London, Oxford and Berlin. He left an unpromising career as a professional basketball player to study the Romantics – an experience he wrote about in *Playing Days*. Since then he has taught high-school English, worked at a left-wing cultural magazine, and published seven novels, including *Either Side of Winter*, about a New York private school, and a trilogy on the life of Lord Byron: *Imposture*, *A Quiet Adjustment* and *Childish Loves*. His most recent novel, *You Don't Have To Live Like This*, is about an experimental community in Detroit. *Granta* selected him as one of the Best of Young British Novelists in 2013. Markovits lives in London and is married, with a daughter and a son. He teaches Creative Writing at Royal Holloway, University of London.

PARTOU ZIA emigrated to England from Tehran in 1970, at the age of twelve. She studied Art History at the University of Warwick (1977–80) and Fine Art at the Slade (1986–91). In 1993 she moved to Cornwall, where she lived and worked until her death from cancer in March 2008. Zia married the artist Richard Cook in 2001 and during the last years of her life her painting developed, culminating in an exhibition at Tate St Ives 2003. She was also a prolific author, though her written work was not published in her lifetime.

ANAKANA SCHOFIELD won the Amazon.ca First Novel Award and the Debut-Litzer Prize for Fiction in 2013 for her debut novel *Malarky*. *Malarky* was also nominated for the Ethel Wilson Fiction Prize, selected as a Barnes & Noble Discover Great New Writers pick and named on many Best Book of the Year lists for 2012 and 2013. *Martin John*, her critically acclaimed second novel, was shortlisted for the Giller Prize and the Ethel Wilson Fiction Prize. Schofield contributes criticism and essays to the *London Review of Books* blog, the *Guardian*, the Irish Times, the *Globe and Mail* and more.

nh Notting Hill Editions

Notting Hill Editions is devoted to the best in essay writing. Our authors, living and dead, cover a broad range of non-fiction, but all display the virtues of brevity, soul and wit.

Our commitment to reinvigorating the essay as a literary form extends to our website, where we host the wonderful Essay Library, a home for the world's most important and enjoyable essays, including the facility to search, save your favourites and add your comments and suggestions.

To discover more, please visit
www.nottinghilleditions.com

Other titles in the Series*

On Dolls
edited by Kenneth Gross

The essays in this collection explore the seriousness of play and the mysteries of inanimate life – the 'unknown spaces, dust, lost objects, and small animals that fill any house'. *On Dolls* includes contributions from Baudelaire, Rilke, Freud, Elizabeth Bishop and Marina Warner.

Still Life with a Bridle
by Zbigniew Herbert

A gathering of artful essays by one of Poland's most translated writers. Poet and essayist Zbigniew Herbert takes an intriguing look at the cultural, artistic and aesthetic legacy of 17th-century Holland.

'Herbert is one of the finest and most original writers in Europe.'
– *The New Yorker*

Triptych: Three Studies after Francis Bacon
by Jonathan Litell

Francis Bacon was one of the iconic figures of modern art, who transformed the way we see and experience the human body. Mirroring Bacon's famous triptychs, Littell's three essays engage with the artist's contorted figures, his screaming popes and apes, his flanks of beef and his umbrellas. Illustrated with 25 colour images.

CLASSIC COLLECTION

The Classic Collection brings together the finest essayists of the past, introduced by contemporary writers.

Grumbling at Large – Selected Essays of J. B. Priestley
Introduced by Valerie Grove

Beautiful and Impossible Things
– Selected Essays of Oscar Wilde
Introduced by Gyles Brandreth

Words of Fire – Selected Essays of Ahad Ha'am
Introduced by Brian Klug

Essays on the Self – Selected Essays of Virginia Woolf
Introduced by Joanna Kavenna

All That is Worth Remembering
– Selected Essays of William Hazlitt
Introduced by Duncan Wu

*All NHE titles are available in the UK, and some titles are available in the rest of the world. For more information, please visit www.nottinghilleditions.com.

A selection of our titles are distributed in the US and Canada by New York Review Books. For more information on available titles, please visit www.nyrb.com.

NS